D0591719

PRESENTED TO:

_____

FROM:

_____

Spirit CALLING

HAL & CARLA WHITE
BOYD BAILEY

iDisciple | Publishing

INTRODUCTION

My first step in the journey of experiencing the presence of God was in 1981 when I read *The Practice of the Presence of God* by Brother Lawrence. The book encouraged me to develop the practice—or habit—of maintaining a continual awareness of the presence of God. What struck me most was the depth of Lawrence's love for God. I was beginning to understand that God desires an intimate relationship with us, which is cultivated by recognizing He is with us every moment of every day. The truth is we can learn to become consciously aware of the continual presence of God.

My second experience in practicing the presence of God was through a small group of men I met with every other week for two years. We connected relationally and had conversations about who God created us to be and how to learn to hear the quiet, still prompting of His Spirit. We explored how to experience God's love and how to develop habits to discern an awareness of the Spirit's presence every day in our lives. The entire focus and goal of our time together was to lead us into a more intimate relationship with God, Jesus, and the Holy Spirit. It was on a weekend retreat with these men where I felt the nudging of the Spirit to write a devotional to help people experience intimacy with Him and to discover the resource He gave us—the Holy Spirit. It is through the power of the Spirit that we are able to abide in and walk with God. We can learn to keep in step with the Spirit and to live in His power, but it takes practice.

As I was praying through the prompting to write this book, I met with a friend I've known for many years. I revealed how God was strongly impressing me to share what I was learning about living in His presence and relying on the often neglected and misunderstood power of the Spirit. To my utter amazement, my friend, Boyd, had been wrestling with the same prompting and had been journaling about the Spirit for quite some time. In fact, he had recently had a conversation with his son-in-law about what to do with this desire to share what he was learning about the Spirit. We committed to pray about this desire God placed in each of our hearts individually and collectively, which is what led to the book you are now holding in your hands.

Spirit Calling was written to encourage you to intentionally reflect on the Spirit and His leading in your life. Each daily reading begins with a Scripture and is written in the voice of your heavenly Father—as if is He is speaking directly to you. The words we penned are not inerrant and do not carry the authority of Scripture. They are simply written as if you were sitting alone with your heavenly Father—the One who knows you best and loves you most—and listening to Him lovingly share His thoughts with you.

Our hope and prayer is for you to carve out time each day to sit with your heavenly Father, tuning out all outside voices and giving your undivided attention to the God who uniquely created you and extravagantly loves you. As you spend time with Him in His Word and reflect on the *Spirit Calling* daily reading, we encourage you to ask the Holy Spirit to lead you into the presence of the Father and reveal His thoughts to you and to write those thoughts down. With your Bible, journal, and *Spirit Calling* in your lap, we encourage you to take a deep breath, exhale, and wait for God as you invite Him to speak to you through His Spirit.

The Spirit is calling!

Hal White

JANUARY

*The Spirit you received
does not make you slaves,
so that you live in fear again;
rather, the Spirit you
received brought about your
adoption to sonship.*

ROMANS 8:15

Now the earth was formless and empty,
darkness was over the surface of the deep.

GENESIS 1:2

TRUST ME. At times, you will feel darkness over the face of your faith, but you can trust Me to create form out of void and to give fullness in places of emptiness. I have always been. I was in the beginning of creation, and I am working in and through you to complete My work of grace. My Spirit strengthens your spirit to enable you to walk in My power. I am at work creating good things for you, My beloved child.

Spirit of God, when my faith is weak, remind me that You are working in and through me, creating fullness out of emptiness. Give me strength and empower me to follow You.

. . . and the Spirit of God was
hovering over the waters.

GENESIS 1:2

MY SPIRIT HOVERS OVER YOUR LIFE and dwells in you. I hover over your life with My loving presence. I hover over your heart with My purity and protection. I hover over your mind with My revelation and wisdom. I hover over your relationships with My forgiveness and grace. I know what you need. My Spirit is always present to lead and guide you through good times and challenging times. His peaceful presence calms any anxious thoughts weighing you down.

Spirit of God, hover over my heart, mind, and life and guide me into perfect peace.

I will give you a new heart and put a
new spirit in you; I will remove from you your
heart of stone and give you a heart of flesh.

EZEKIEL 36:26

LISTEN TO ME and let My words soften your heart. When you steal away from the distractions of the day and spend time with Me, My Spirit molds your heart to be like Mine. I long for you to trust and rely on Me because you know Me rather than out of a religious obligation. Take time today to look for evidence of Me working in you—even in the smallest ways. Let Me turn your heart of stone into a heart that longs for Me. There's nothing more I want than your heart.

Holy Spirit, fashion my heart after my Father's heart. Create in me an unquenchable desire to know You and rest in Your presence.

If you are led by the Spirit,
you are not under the law.

GALATIANS 5:18

INTIMACY WITH ME is so much more than rules and regulations. Trying to please Me based on "Do this!" or "Don't
do that!" leads to performance-based religiosity. My love
for you is not based on how good you are. I am interested
in *who* you are rather than *what* you do. I love you unconditionally, with no strings attached. My beloved, slow
down and focus your attention on how deeply I love you
just for who you are. Trying to attain spiritual perfection
by keeping the law will only lead to exhaustion. The Holy
Spirit is the only source of power for you to live freely,
abundantly, and victoriously.

Holy Spirit, I yield to You and give myself wholly to
Your guidance.

The LORD will guide you always;
he will satisfy your needs in a sun-scorched land
and will strengthen your frame.
You will be like a well-watered garden,
like a spring whose waters never fail.

ISAIAH 58:11

THE SPIRIT IS YOUR GUIDE. He leads you through all of life's circumstances. He guides you in rejoicing and sorrow. He guides you in success and when you face difficulty. He guides you in times of plenty and in times of scarcity. In times of lack, I provide your daily bread. I hear your cries to Me when you are spiritually dry or emotionally empty. My Spirit waters your soul to refresh and restore you. My Word brings relief and quenches your parched heart with love and hope. My Spirit is your living water—an eternal spring creating a stream leading directly to your heart.

Heavenly Father, thank You for guiding me through each and every circumstance I face. There is nothing better than Your refreshing living water when I am dry and empty. Fill me to overflowing with hope and love as I trust You in the midst of adversity. Only by Your power can I overcome fear and live in freedom.

You will show me the path that leads to life;
your presence fills me with joy
and brings me pleasure forever.

PSALM 16:11, GNT

THE PATH THAT LEADS TO LIFE is found in Me. Each morning, I wait for you to connect with Me and refresh yourself in My presence. I long to be invited to come alongside you during your day—to be invited into the big moments and the minutiae of your day. I want to be a part of everything you do today. You will find true joy in My presence, as well as comfort, strength, peace, and so much more! You are filled with joy and hope by the power of the Holy Spirit living in you. Be completely confident that I am always with you—waiting on the sideline to be invited into each moment of your day.

Heavenly Father, remind me to seek joy in Your presence in the midst of all the distractions of my day. Show me the way to the path that leads to life, and when I find it, I know You will be waiting for me.

I waited patiently for the Lord;
he turned to me and heard my cry.

PSALM 40:1

WAITING IS SO VERY DIFFICULT. You live in a world of quick fixes and instant gratification. You have been trained to expect immediate responses, but My response is not always—in fact, most often is not—instant. I see you losing faith and becoming fearful of the unknown. My child, this is when you need to trust Me, watch for Me, and wait for Me. Your natural tendency is to outrun Me and make your own way, but I want you to grow and mature spiritually. The Spirit needs space and time to work in your heart to help you let go of fear and allow your circumstances to teach you. Prayer is My gift to you—the gift of communion with Me. I hear your cry, and the answer is on the way. Sit with Me as you patiently wait for My answer.

Heavenly Father, forgive me when I hurry the process and run ahead of You. Teach me what it means to have faith in the silence. Help me to become more patient so I can have hope that doesn't die and perseverance that doesn't quit.

The mind governed by the flesh is death,
but the mind governed by the Spirit is life and peace.

ROMANS 8:6

THE WORLD COMPETES FOR EVERY SINGLE THOUGHT you have. You are constantly bombarded with messages in what you read, watch, and hear. Mixed messages avalanche your mind, and many are negative and void of Me. They lead you to spiritual and emotional death. I, too, speak to you. My Spirit's subtle whisper in your heart, the beauty of a sunset, or a Scripture that comes to mind out of nowhere are all ways I speak to you. My messages are life-giving: they flood you with peace. When you feel discouraged, depressed, anxious, or fearful, I invite you to pull away from everything to be with Me, and I will cover you with My presence. My Spirit will set your mind on life and fill you with peace and hope.

Holy Spirit, transform my thought life by Your power,
keeping my mind on You and controlling my thoughts.
Fill me with life and peace as I set my mind on You.

The LORD is my strength and my shield;
my heart trusts in him, and he helps me.
My heart leaps for joy,
and with my song I praise him.

PSALM 28:7

I AM YOUR PLACE OF REFUGE. When your world shatters, I pick up the pieces and hold them in My hands. My Spirit comforts you in your distress and gives you the strength to carry on. He shines a light of hope into the deep crevices of your heart. You can trust Me to take the broken pieces of your life and put them back together. As I heal your heart, I breathe life into your soul. I am a master craftsman, and I will renovate you from the inside out. I make beauty out of ashes and redeem what is lost.

Heavenly Father, thank You for holding the shattered pieces of my life in Your hands when my world falls apart. I trust You to redeem me and make me into something more beautiful than I was so I can boast of the master craftsman that You are.

*I pray that out of his glorious riches he may strengthen you
with power through his spirit in your inner being,
so that Christ may dwell in your hearts through faith.*

EPHESIANS 3:16–17

MY SPIRIT GIVES YOU STRENGTH when you face temptations that are impossible to resist on your own. Cling to Me when trials leave you hopeless and scared. Trust Me when financial struggles threaten to drown you. Take My hand and listen to My voice so I can teach you with each step. Sometimes I speak loudly, but there are times when I drop My voice to a low whisper so you will learn to discern My voice above the clatter of your trials. Lean into Me and let Me walk you through the challenges you encounter. Soak up each word I pour into you along the journey. One day I will ask you to take the hand of someone facing similar circumstances to walk them along the path we forged together. As always, I will be your strength and encouragement as you lead others to Me.

Holy Spirit, help me to hear Your voice and follow Your leading in my life. Thank You that Your power strengthens me so I can use what You've taught me to help others on their journey.

So I say, walk by the Spirit,
and you will not gratify the desires of the flesh.

GALATIANS 5:16

I KNOW THIS EARTHLY LIFE IS FULL OF ENTICEMENTS that pull for your attention. My desire is for you to long for Me instead—to place Me at the forefront of your thoughts and affections. As you walk by the power of the Spirit, you will tap into My unlimited strength and guidance. Put Me above yourself in all things. It will be difficult, but it will lead to a more full, abundant, and fulfilling life. When you feel pulled in opposite directions, listen carefully and take heed as My Spirit guides you into My will. This will become more natural the longer we walk together. Take My hand and walk with Me.

Holy Spirit, help me to be conscious of my decisions since I am prone to being pulled away by people and situations that seem appealing to me. Teach me to know Your voice and follow You above all others and allow You to lead me to higher ground.

Flesh gives birth to flesh,
but the Spirit gives birth to spirit.

JOHN 3:6

BECAUSE YOU WERE BORN OF THE FLESH of your parents, you were born a natural man. As such, you were born incapable of loving, obeying, or knowing Me. Your spiritual transformation took place when you put your trust in Me and I filled you with My Spirit. Now that you have been born of the Spirit, you will come to resemble Me. Just as a child bears the name of his parent, you will bear My name. What a joy to be transformed from carnal and corrupt to redeemed and sanctified, from spiritually undiscerning to someone who draws on My wisdom, and from walking in darkness to being welcomed into My very presence. Rejoice, My child! Oh, what an inheritance you have received.

Heavenly Father, I lift up my hands in praise to You. You redeemed my soul, and I am forever changed. You gave me Your name, and I am eternally grateful.

*He who searches our hearts knows the mind
of the Spirit, because the Spirit intercedes for God's
people in accordance with the will of God.*

ROMANS 8:27

I SEARCH YOUR HEART and know your deep desires.
Pour out your heart, and the Spirit will intercede for you.
When you don't know what to pray, the Spirit will come
to Me on your behalf. The Spirit will ask what you may
not be aware to ask and will plead with Me for mercy in
ways that are unattainable for you. Come with a humble
heart and a spirit willing to yield to Me, and then, My
child, rest in knowing that I am working on your behalf.

*Spirit of God, I praise You for interceding for me with
power and wisdom that I do not have. I yield my will to
Yours. Thank You for interceding on my behalf, guiding
me as I align my life to God's will.*

Since we live by the Spirit,
let us keep in step with the Spirit.

GALATIANS 5:25

ALLOW ME TO WALK WITH YOU through this life. There will be times you are tempted to walk at your own pace, set your own stride, and move ahead of Me. Hold My hand and keep in step with Me. This is a choice you must make daily, even moment by moment. Following your own way may feel good but will ultimately lead to a dead-end path full of thorns and dry land. When you allow My Spirit to lead you, your selfish desires will no longer have control over you, and you will finally experience true freedom. I will always guide you in the right direction. Trust Me to lead you as you walk in step with Me.

Oh, Holy Spirit, how I long to follow You each and every moment of my life. When the choice is difficult and the pull to go my own way is strong, help me to remember that keeping in step with You results in a much smoother walk and a more rewarding destination.

JANUARY 15

If you then, though you are evil,
know how to give good gifts to your children,
how much more will your Father in heaven give
the Holy Spirit to those who ask him!

LUKE 11:13

THERE ARE TIMES WHEN YOU WILL BE SCARED and lonely. When you don't know which way to turn, ask My Spirit for guidance. When it feels too difficult to take the next step, ask the Spirit for strength. When you are tempted to believe you can do life on your own, ask the Spirit for an awareness of your need for Me. Be still in My presence and receive a fresh supply of My grace and power. I long to fill you with My Spirit. There is no better gift than the blessings I give you through the Spirit. Ask and receive, for I love you so.

Heavenly Father, awaken my soul to You each and every day. I am unworthy yet so thankful for the gift of Your Spirit and His power in my life. He is evidence that You are my good, good Father.

JANUARY 16

Dear friends, do not believe every spirit,
but test the spirits to see whether
they are from God, because many false prophets
have gone out into the world.

1 JOHN 4:1

YOU ARE LIKE A SHEEP in a world of wolves. My Spirit will put a hedge of protection around you and lead you to the truth. There will be so many voices claiming to speak truth, but I am the source of all truth. When you turn to Me, I will clear up confusion and guide you to truth. Don't let backbiting and bickering unravel you. Bring your questions and concerns to Me, and ask the Spirit to make My ways known to you. The more you come to know Me, the more you will know and understand My great love for you; and out of My unlimited love for you, love the people I place in your life.

Heavenly Father, I don't want to be easily influenced and deceived into believing lies about You. Give me a hunger to know Your Word and discernment to understand Your truth. Protect me from any influence that is not from You.

When the day of Pentecost came, they were all together in one place. Suddenly a sound like the blowing of a violent wind came from heaven and filled the whole house where they were sitting.

ACTS 2:1–2

THERE WILL BE TIMES IN LIFE when you feel an intense longing for My Spirit. Sometimes He will simply come and share your space, whispering words of encouragement, direction, and hope. Other times He will choose to swoop in with a mighty force, filling you afresh with His power. Open your heart, soul, and mind to Him when He comes in power to free you from the shackles of bondage and apathy that hold you back from the abundant life I have for you. His power is as available to you today as it was to My disciples. Just as I used them to make My name known, I want to use you to accomplish great and mighty things for My kingdom.

Holy Spirit, I invite You into my heart, soul, and mind. Clear the cobwebs of apathy and disbelief and ignite in me a passion and zeal to make known Your saving grace and unconditional love. Embolden me with a fresh filling of Your powerful Spirit.

Praise be to the God and Father of our Lord Jesus Christ,
the Father of compassion and the God of all comfort,
who comforts us in all our troubles, so that we can
comfort those in any trouble with the comfort
we ourselves receive from God.

2 CORINTHIANS 1:3–4

COMFORT AND COMPASSION ARE MY SPECIALTY. When you are overcome with grief, I grieve with you. When you are brokenhearted, I come close to you. When sorrow paralyzes you, the Spirit covers you in comfort and intercedes on your behalf. I wrap My loving arms around you and embrace you with compassion. Bring your raw emotions to Me—over and over again—as grief ebbs and flows in your heart. I will hold your hand as you travel the path of pain and heartache. In time, My light will break through the darkness that shrouds you, and I will walk with you into new hope, where I make beauty out of ashes.

My greatest comfort in the midst of my most difficult days is knowing there is purpose in my pain. God of all comfort, meet me in my grief so I can mirror Your comfort and compassion when You intersect my path with those who are hurting.

Do not conform to the pattern of this world,
but be transformed by the renewing of your mind. Then you
will be able to test and approve what
God's will is—his good, pleasing and perfect will.

ROMANS 12:2

YOU ARE ALWAYS GOING TO FEEL a pull toward the world and away from Me. This world offers many enticements and opportunities that seem undeniably exciting at the time. The indwelling Spirit will help you distinguish My will from yours when you spend time with Me and in My Word. When you need to make a decision, draw on the words the Spirit whispers in your soul. The gentle nudge of My Spirit will warn you of danger and temptations. I want the very best for your life and will always provide a way to resist those things that will lure you away from Me. Gather strength from the power of My Spirit to avoid distractions that keep you from My perfect plan for your life.

Heavenly Father, I often find myself lured in by the things of this world. Help me to listen to Your Spirit and to distinguish between good and evil.

JANUARY 20

The Spirit of God has made me;
the breath of the Almighty gives me life.

JOB 33:4

MY SPIRIT BREATHES LIFE INTO YOU—both physical life and spiritual life. I am the air you breathe, and I want to breathe fresh air into your soul. I will lead you out of the cycle of self-dependence and apathy into a life of passion, purpose, and hope. Bring your pain to Me. Bring your dreams to Me. Let Me show you the way to go. When you come to the end of yourself, turn to Me. I will show you who you are in Christ. My Spirit will renew your strength and lead you to dependence on Me. As you surrender, I will use your past and present to create a life of beauty and love.

Heavenly Father, I want to live a life of purpose and hope in You. Anything less is a cheap counterfeit. Help me to allow Your Spirit to live through me.

I am the good shepherd,
and I know My own,
and My own know Me.

JOHN 10:14, NASB

LISTEN CLOSELY to the whisper of My voice, for I know you intimately. Bring your troubled heart to Me, and I will shepherd you through difficult times and tempting situations. Trust My Spirit to lead you, even when it is uncomfortable and confining. When you are tempted to wander, My divine Spirit will provide, protect, defend, guide, guard, and lead you. Hear My voice and follow Me.

Heavenly Father, help me to discern the voice of Your Spirit and follow You. In You I will find protection, guidance, and provision.

I keep asking that the God of our Lord Jesus Christ,
the glorious Father, may give you the Spirit of wisdom
and revelation, so that you may know him better.

EPHESIANS 1:17

I DESIGNED YOU and will provide you with exactly what you need when you need it. My Spirit will give you wisdom and discernment to navigate whatever circumstances or problems you face. Draw upon My infinite wisdom. Trust and depend on the Spirit for revelation into the problems you are wrestling with right now—in your home, in your business, in your marriage, and with your children. In Me, you will find purpose and hope. Keep asking, and I will show you more of My wisdom and more of Myself.

Heavenly Father, my heart longs for You. Thank You for providing all that I need to navigate this life. Lead me into wisdom as I serve You with all that I am.

All whose hearts were stirred and whose spirits were moved
came and brought their sacred offerings to the Lord.

EXODUS 35:21, NLT

I FREELY GIVE TO YOU so you can open your hands and freely give to others. The way of the world tells you that all you have is for you, but the path of greed will leave you unfulfilled, empty, and discontent. As you loosen your grip on your life and possessions and take hold of a life of generosity, you will experience freedom. You will experience fulfillment and joy as your heart becomes more like Mine. When you give generously and graciously, you imitate Me and demonstrate who I am. You will discover that it truly is more of a blessing to give than to receive.

Oh, Heavenly Father, You are so generous to me! May Your Spirit give me open hands and an open heart to give generously and reflect You to those around me.

Commit to the LORD whatever you do,
and he will establish your plans.

PROVERBS 16:3

MY WILL FOR YOU IS FULL OF POSSIBILITIES that take time to develop. I know it is difficult for you to wait on Me, but I will give you a secure future full of hope if you will trust Me to lead you. I want you to experience the fullness of who I am and what I have for you. Don't settle for less. You will live with purpose and significance as you rely on the Holy Spirit to show you My best plan for your life.

Heavenly Father, I want to follow Your path and plan for my life. Give me guardrails to keep me on course and patience to persevere as I follow You.

*Because my servant Caleb has a different spirit
and follows me wholeheartedly, I will bring him into
the land he went to, and his descendants will inherit it.*

NUMBERS 14:24

MY SPIRIT WILL GIVE YOU CONFIDENCE to overcome fear and live with assurance. I saved you and set you apart as Mine. I desire your wholehearted love and affection. My heart for you is not to wander around in the wilderness of loving this world, but to follow the Spirit wholeheartedly into a place of spiritual freedom and abundance. The Holy Spirit will give you significance and will help you accomplish My plans for you. Follow Me into a life full of adventure and freedom.

Spirit of God, empower me to wholeheartedly follow You. Give me eyes to see the adventure of living a life fully surrendered to You.

Posterity will serve him;
future generations will be told about the Lord.

PSALM 22:30

WALKING IN TRUTH brings you great blessing and brings Me great joy. My Holy Spirit indwells you to inspire and instruct your family for generations to come, and your children benefit from your willingness to fully follow Me. It pleases Me when you leave behind a legacy of love for Me. I smile when I see you serve in a way that leads the next generation to passionately follow Me. The best gift you can give your children is to model living by faith and trusting Me.

Heavenly Father, help me to live in the power of the Spirit to lead the next generation to follow You.

For the word of God is alive and active.
Sharper than any double-edged sword,
it penetrates even to dividing soul and spirit,
joints and marrow; it judges the thoughts
and attitudes of the heart.

HEBREWS 4:12

YOU CAN TAKE ME AT MY WORD. I do not slur or stutter. Holy Scripture is a sure word from Me and is living and active. My voice is a tender whisper that soothes your spirit, a caring correction that advises your conscience, or a loud warning over foolishness. Receive My sacred Word to show you how to become more like Me and to live for Me.

Heavenly Father, lead my heart and mind through Your living Word to make me more like You.

The righteous cry out, and the LORD hears them;
he delivers them from all their troubles.

PSALM 34:17

MY BELOVED, I WILL SEE YOU as you walk through the dark night of your soul. The Spirit is like a guiding light, leading you toward the daybreak of hope. Grasp My hand of grace and walk with Me, though fear may slow your steps nearly to a stop. My grace is sufficient for one step at a time. Bask in the light of My radiant presence as My Spirit leads you to take one step at a time, and I will deliver you from all your troubles.

Spirit of God, thank You for always hearing my cries. Teach me to stay in step with You, even during my darkest days.

JANUARY 29

The LORD sustains them on their sickbed
and restores them from their bed of illness.

PSALM 41:3

MY HEART ACHES when you experience physical suffering. I uniquely created your body, so when you cringe in pain, I feel your pain. I am intimate with each and every blood vessel and organ inside you. I knit you together in your mother's womb, creating the intricate cellular structure in your skin and bones. I have embedded in your body defensive means to defeat disease. All your ailments are My concern. When you suffer, My Spirit will comfort and sustain you and restore your soul.

Heavenly Father, I'm grateful that Your Spirit sustains me when I suffer. Give me strength to glorify You not only on my best days, but also on my worst. I entrust myself to Your loving care.

JANUARY 30

Therefore we do not lose heart.
Though outwardly we are wasting away,
yet inwardly we are being renewed day by day.
For our light and momentary troubles are achieving
for us an eternal glory that far outweighs them all.

2 CORINTHIANS 4:16-17

DO NOT FEAR SICKNESS AND DISEASE. Put your confidence, hope, security, and joy in Me. I know your deepest desires. The Spirit is with you and will not forsake you in your time of need. I will restore you for My glory on earth, or I will heal you for eternal life in heaven. Do not lose heart! I am renewing you every day. None of your pain is wasted—it is producing an eternal glory that far outweighs your suffering.

Heavenly Father, You know pain better than anyone. Thank You for sustaining me in my suffering. Nothing I experience here on earth compares to eternal life with You.

"Not so, my lord," Hannah replied,
"I am a woman who is deeply troubled.
I have not been drinking wine or beer;
I was pouring out my soul to the LORD."

1 SAMUEL 1:15

TRUST ME in the middle of your overwhelming unmet desires. My child, pour out your soul on the altar of My great mercy and compassion. I feel your aggravation and agitation with having to wait, but don't give up hope. My perfect provision will come to you in My best timing. Yes, My beloved, pour out your soul to Me, and I'll pour out My Spirit and grace on you.

Heavenly Father, I long to live in Your calming presence and perfect peace. I pour out my soul in humble submission as I wait for You.

FEBRUARY

The fruit of the Spirit is love,
joy, peace, patience, kindness,
goodness, faithfulness, gentleness,
self-control; against such things
there is no law.

GALATIANS 5:22–23, ESV

Now the Lord is the Spirit, and where the
Spirit of the Lord is, there is freedom.

2 CORINTHIANS 3:17

LIFE AND LIBERTY ARE FOUND IN MY SPIRIT. Come to Me when you are depressed, anxious, discouraged, confused, or oppressed so that My Spirit can lead you out of bondage and into freedom. In your confusion, My Spirit gives clarity and wisdom. In your anger, seek His calming presence. In your frustration, seek My face in prayer. Living by faith may cause others to see you as irrational, but I love to see you walking in faith by the power of the Spirit. Freedom is found in My Spirit.

Heavenly Father, I celebrate freedom in Your Spirit. Draw near to me when my emotions begin to take over. Give me the strength and courage to live for You.

Blessed are those who hunger and thirst for righteousness, for they will be satisfied.

MATTHEW 5:6, NASB

RIGHTEOUSNESS LEADS TO SATISFACTION. My Spirit creates a hunger for Me and My agenda for your life. It's easy to forget Me in your haste to satisfy your needs, but My Spirit fills and satisfies your soul more deeply and fully than any earthly comfort. If I lead you to deny yourself for a season, lean into the Spirit in prayer for strength. Fast from the noise of a rushed culture and engage with Me in quiet reflection. My Spirit alone can satisfy you.

Heavenly Father, satisfy my soul with Your indwelling Spirit. Fill my deep longings with the nourishment of Your love.

Come to me, all you who are weary and burdened,
and I will give you rest.

MATTHEW 11:28

I SEE BENEATH THE SURFACE of your heart and soul. When you walk without Me, you become weary and burdened. Your load is too heavy to bear without My Spirit. I invite you to exchange your burdens for My yoke—it is easy and light. Cast your cares upon Me, and you will find rest for your soul. I am gentle and offer freedom and peace. Let Me guide you into sweet relief and rest.

Heavenly Father, I admit that I often take on too much. Prompt me to bring all my burdens and anxieties to You. Teach me how to rest in You.

FEBRUARY 4

What, then, shall we say in response to these things?
If God is for us, who can be against us?

ROMANS 8:31

I AM FOR YOU. I am for your dreams and desires. I am for your family and faith. I am for your work and hobbies. Because I am for you, you can slow down, stop striving, and enter into the joy of our friendship. Your worth is found in Me, and nothing can separate you from My love. My Spirit empowers you to be all I've created you to be. You become fully alive as you rely on the Spirit in dependent faith. Remember, I am for you.

Heavenly Father, it's easy to feel as if I don't measure up. I so often forget You are my biggest supporter and encourager. I desire to be all that You've created me to be, not by striving in my own effort, but by the power of the Spirit.

You have made known to me the paths of life;
you will fill me with joy in your presence.

ACTS 2:28

MY SPIRIT WILL STEER YOU toward My purposes. Where I lead may not always make sense to you, but I will always lead you into a life of meaning and fulfillment. I am in control and fully aware of everything going on in and around you. You can trust Me to know what is best for you, even if it's not always easy. You will never draw a single breath or take a step when I'm not with you. As you spend time with Me and listen to the Spirit, I will make known My path for you.

Heavenly Father, help me to yield to the stirrings of Your Spirit and trust Your plan for my life. Thank You for the promise to never leave me. As long as I have You, I am safe and secure.

You gave your good Spirit to instruct them.
You did not withhold your manna from their mouths,
and you gave them water for their thirst.

NEHEMIAH 9:20

EVERYTHING YOU NEED CAN BE FOUND IN ME. At times I will lead you out of your comfort zone, and you will feel as if you are wandering in the wilderness. Rest in Me and allow My Spirit to light the path and lead you exactly where I want you. I will provide for your every need, oftentimes in unexpected ways. Walking in the power of the Spirit will give you the wisdom and courage to stay the course and follow Me wherever I lead. You can trust Me to sustain you, for I am good.

Heavenly Father, You hold my life together. Help me to be in tune with even the slightest prompting of Your Spirit. Give me the faith to follow wherever You lead.

But when he, the Spirit of truth, comes,
he will guide you into all the truth.
He will not speak on his own;
he will speak only what he hears,
and he will tell you what is yet to come.

JOHN 16:13

MY HOLY SPIRIT IS YOUR ULTIMATE TEACHER of truth and will guide you down the path to reach My destination for you. When you became My child, I gave you My Spirit to empower you with all you need to follow Me, and I lead you in truth based on your needs today. You will be tempted to worry as you look into the future, but worrying about the future will cause you to miss what the Spirit wants to reveal to you today. There is no need to worry, My child, because the Spirit will go before you, leading the way, clearing obstacles, and giving clarity.

Heavenly Father, fill me with Your Holy Spirit to lead me into holy living for You, and grant me the wisdom I need today.

Into Your hand I commit my spirit;
You have ransomed me, O LORD, God of truth.

PSALM 31:5, NASB

MY LOVE RANSOMED YOU from unrighteousness. My Son paid the ransom for your sin, giving you abundant life on earth and eternal life with Me. You can depend on Me alone, for I am faithful and true. I am your refuge and can always be trusted. No one can take what you give to Me. My Spirit seals you in security and keeps you safe. You are all Mine.

Heavenly Father, thank You that Your Spirit seals me in You and nothing can separate me from You.

Jesus answered, "I am the way and the truth and the life.
No one comes to the Father except through me."

JOHN 14:6

I AM THE SPIRIT OF TRUTH, so I can be trusted to lead you into all truth. Do not listen to lies that lead you astray; instead, embrace My good way. Just as a father and mother pray for their child to know, understand, and walk in truth, I also deeply desire this for you, My child. I give you freedom from fear when you trust My love and My truth. I am the way, the truth, and the life.

Heavenly Father, I believe Your Word. My heart's desire is to walk obediently in Your truth. Thank You for opening my eyes to the way, the truth, and the life through Jesus.

For we know, brothers and sisters loved by God,
that he has chosen you, because our gospel came to you not
simply with words but also with power, with the
Holy Spirit and deep conviction. You know how
we lived among you for your sake.

1 THESSALONIANS 1:4–5

MY SPIRIT EMPOWERS YOU to live out the gospel so that others may see Me at work in you. I want to use you to impact the lives of those you work with, play with, and live with each and every day. Your only part is to abide in Me—to connect with Me and relinquish control to the Spirit. The Spirit's part is to produce fruit in you and through you. He will do all the work. The Spirit will produce love, joy, peace, patience, kindness, goodness, faithfulness, gentleness, and self-control in you. You will be a model of My love to those around you.

Heavenly Father, thank You for the privilege of making You known to the people You place in my life. Help me to get out of the way and allow Your Spirit to shine in me and point everyone around me to You.

The fruit of the Spirit is love, joy, peace,
patience, kindness, goodness, faithfulness, gentleness,
self-control; against such things there is no law.

GALATIANS 5:22–23, NASB

MY LOVE IS FOUNDATIONAL. My Spirit empowers you to love others as I love you. Love is how people will know you belong to Me—it gives you authentic affection for Me and for the people you meet each day. I have an endless supply of love for you. Love is patient and kind, and it offers comfort. In the same way I love and care for you, allow My Spirit to love and care for others through you.

Heavenly Father, grow my capacity to receive and give Your abundant love. Show me opportunities each day to shower those around me with Your amazing love.

Over all these virtues put on love,
which binds them all together in perfect unity.

COLOSSIANS 3:14

LOVE DOESN'T DIVIDE, it unifies. Love doesn't take, it gives. Love is not selfish, it is selfless. The Holy Spirit empowers you to love others. The more time you spend in My presence, the more I can saturate you in My love. There is no force more powerful than My love. I want to heal your wounded heart, transform your life, and free you from sin and shame with My unfailing, unconditional love. You are not capable of loving beyond human effort without strength from My Spirit. The Spirit gives you the power to love like Me—to pray for your enemies, embrace your critics, forgive all who hurt you, and honor your parents with My unconditional love.

Heavenly Father, help me to grasp how wide and long and high and deep Your love is for me. Thank You for Christ's sacrifice—the ultimate demonstration of Your perfect love. Let Your love flow freely through me by Your Spirit so I can love others the way You love me.

If you love those who love you, what credit is that to you?
Even sinners love those who love them.

LUKE 6:32

MY LOVE COVERS ALL SIN. There is no one beyond the reach of My love. Loving those you consider undeserving or unlovable can only be accomplished through the power of the Spirit. When you love someone who does not love back, rejoice as you remember that this is how I loved you. As your relationship with Me develops, your love for Me and others will increase. The Spirit makes a way for you to share who I am with those who are difficult to love. Loving others is the greatest display of My presence in your life.

Heavenly Father, thank You for loving me when I was undeserving and unlovable. Give me eyes to see people the way You view them. I want to be known for loving people the way You love me.

A new command I give you: Love one another.
As I have loved you, so you must love one another.

JOHN 13:34

YOU LOVE BECAUSE I FIRST LOVED YOU. Everything hangs on My love. If you love Me and love others as I have loved you, everything else will fall into place. It sounds so easy, but it's impossible when you try to do it in your own strength. I don't ask you to love out of your own ability, but through the Spirit living in you. I will love people through you. The Spirit is a permanent deposit in you and wants to empower you to live a new way—My way. The Spirit will empower you to love people with My love—because I see their pain, their fear, their insecurity—and I want you to love them like I love them.

Heavenly Father, thank You for loving me with a radical love that made me new. Let Your love bubble up and spill out of me onto others and point them to You.

The fruit of the Spirit is love, joy, peace, patience,
kindness, goodness, faithfulness, gentleness, self-control;
against such things there is no law.

GALATIANS 5:22–23, NASB

MY PEACE IS A GIFT TO YOU. My Holy Spirit is a permanent source of peace available to you. When your circumstances swirl with uncertainty, I supply an inner peace to remind you that I am in control. It is a calm that only the Spirit can create. My peace is like a compass for your soul. When you are faced with decisions, a lack of peace is My protection to prevent you from moving forward too fast; it is a check and balance to impulsive, emotional commitments. Peace produced by the Spirit is not subject to shifting situations. Unwrap the gift of My peace and guard your heart and mind through prayer.

Heavenly Father, I rest in Your peaceful presence and trust in You to calm the cares of my heart. Teach me to discern how Your peace can lead me to Your ways.

Finally, brothers and sisters, rejoice, mend your ways,
be comforted, be like-minded, live in peace;
and the God of love and peace will be with you.

2 CORINTHIANS 13:11, NASB

MY PEACE ENABLES YOU TO BE A PEACEMAKER, not just a peacekeeper. My Spirit gives you wisdom to get to the heart of an issue rather than just getting through an issue. My Spirit in you restores broken relationships, brings hurting people together, and creates an atmosphere of harmony. Conflict is inevitable, and the path to peace can be difficult. Don't cheat yourself and others by settling for a counterfeit form of peace. Allow the Spirit to navigate you down a path to true peace. The Spirit's peace within you creates a safe environment of love and acceptance for those in turmoil. Usher in My presence and be one of My peacemakers.

Heavenly Father, I want to be a peacemaker whose peace rests in Your love for me. Give me wisdom and perseverance to withstand the desire to flee rather than allowing Your Spirit to help me resolve conflict.

Peace I leave with you; my peace I give you.
I do not give to you as the world gives.
Do not let your hearts be troubled and do not be afraid.

JOHN 14:27

MY PEACE IS FOUND IN RESTING in a right relationship with Me. I have a never-ending supply of peace for you. My Spirit replaces your chaos with My calming care. Trust conquers anxiety. Tranquility triumphs over striving. My grace removes guilt, leaving behind a renewed sense of your purpose and passion. My peace stands up to the assaults of trouble and fear. I am your refuge, always ready to protect your heart. Receive and rest in My peace.

Prince of Peace, cultivate Your peace in me so that I may rest in Your peaceful presence.

FEBRUARY 18

You will keep in perfect peace those whose minds
are steadfast, because they trust in you.

ISAIAH 26:3

WHEN YOU NEED PEACE, meditate on My thoughts. As you focus on Me, the Spirit will recalibrate your mind and remind you of the big picture and vision I have for your life. When fear of the future overwhelms you, come to Me to replace your anxious thoughts with the assurance of My provision and protection. Bring your worry and anxiety to Me in exchange for My peace. As you surrender to My ways, My Spirit will fill you with peace.

Heavenly Father, renew my mind with Your Spirit's perfect peace as I trust in You with imperfect faith. Prompt me to meditate on You and Your Word when my heart and mind wander from Your truth.

"For my thoughts are not your thoughts, neither are your ways my ways," declares the LORD. "As the heavens are higher than the earth, so are my ways higher than your ways and my thoughts than your thoughts."

ISAIAH 55:8–9

MY WAYS ARE NOT YOUR WAYS, which is why you are in desperate need of being filled with the Spirit. My Spirit will equip you to handle any circumstance you encounter. When you are wronged, the Spirit will prevent you from retaliating. My grace and mercy offer relief instead of demanding a justifiable payment of a debt. I am a gentle Shepherd who guides you with goodness and kindness. My ways are not your ways. My way is the way to abundant life.

Heavenly Father, I desperately need You. Lead me into abundant life and teach me to treat others as You treat me.

As servants of God we commend ourselves
in every way: in great endurance; in troubles,
hardships and distresses.

2 CORINTHIANS 6:4

TRUST IN MY DEEP RESERVOIR OF GRACE to help bear your heavy burdens. I have an endless supply of grace for your physical and emotional suffering. My Spirit will sustain you under the pressures that threaten to crush your confidence. Critics will come and go. Allow difficult circumstances to soften your heart and produce a harvest of righteousness for Me. Your obedience and reliance on Me will encourage other people in their faith.

Heavenly Father, help me to persevere in Your abundant grace and love under the stress of life's pressures so that I can declare Your faithfulness.

Create in me a pure heart, O God,
and renew a steadfast spirit within me.

PSALM 51:10

COME TO ME each and every day and talk to Me. Tell Me where you struggle. I already know these things, but as you share with Me, the Spirit will give you the wisdom to know how to do things differently. I will take your heart and wipe it clean, giving you a fresh start and a new determination. Keep walking and talking with Me. Never give up. Keep going, My child.

Heavenly Father, give me the courage to completely turn my heart over to You each morning. I am overwhelmed by Your unconditional love and forgiveness. Thank You for giving me a fresh start each and every day.

*If the Spirit of him who raised Jesus from the dead
is living in you, he who raised Christ from the dead
will also give life to your mortal bodies because
of his Spirit who lives in you.*

ROMANS 8:11

YOU BELONG TO ME. You are no longer a servant to sin or a slave to fear. You are all Mine; I bought you with a price to live a life of freedom. My power is available to you through the Holy Spirit. The Spirit will help you climb out of your emotional caves of isolation where you hide and walk into My light. Move forward in confidence knowing that you are secure in Me, and I am your source of strength. The Spirit lives in you and enables you to live boldly for Me. Enjoy living in My freedom.

Heavenly Father, I am in awe that the same power that raised Jesus from the dead lives inside me. Teach me to tap into Your power and walk in step with Your Spirit. I praise You that I am no longer a slave to fear.

A servant of the Lord must not quarrel but
must be kind to everyone, be able to teach,
and be patient with difficult people. Gently instruct
those who oppose the truth. Perhaps God will change
those people's hearts, and they will learn the truth.

2 TIMOTHY 2:24–25, NLT

DIFFICULT PEOPLE CAUSE TURMOIL AND STRIFE for you, but I am kind and gentle with you. When you serve those who are difficult in the power of the Spirit with peace, kindness, patience, and gentleness, you represent Me well. I came for the sick and lost, not the healthy. Just as I loved you into a relationship with Me, I want those who are far from Me to come to know Me too. You can trust My Spirit to equip you through the challenges of loving the lost and sharing the hope of My saving grace. He supplies you with wisdom to offer hope and life, and in doing so, reminds you of My goodness and faithfulness as well.

Heavenly Father, I know that Your Spirit alone can open the eyes of the lost and turn them from darkness to light, but I ask You to use me to lead them to You. Prompt me to gently share Your truth and rely on Your power to represent You well.

The woman came and knelt before him.
"Lord, help me!" she said.

MATTHEW 15:25

I AM YOUR REFUGE AND STRENGTH, an ever-present help in trouble. Cry out to Me with all that concerns you and the deep desires of your soul. I see your humble, broken heart. Relational conflict may bruise your emotions, but My love brings healing. Invite Me into your wounded heart with hopeful praise. The Spirit intercedes on your behalf and prays for what you do not know to pray for according to My will. Call on Me, and My mercy and grace will sustain you.

Spirit of God, speak on my behalf. Speak the words my heart cries out, yet I am unable to communicate. Flood me with Your grace and mercy so that I may become whole in You.

*May the God of hope fill you with all joy and peace
as you trust in him, so that you may overflow with hope
by the power of the Holy Spirit.*

ROMANS 15:13

I OFFER YOU HOPE when things appear hopeless. As you spend time communing with Me, you discover that I am trustworthy. When you rely on and trust Me, your faith brings joy in the midst of suffering and peace during the storms of life. My Holy Spirit empowers you to remain firm in your faith and overflow with hope even in the midst of pain, loss, and tragedy.

Heavenly Father, You are my hope! Fill me to overflowing with joy and peace as I learn to completely trust You by the power of the Holy Spirit.

*So he said to me, "This is the word of the L*ORD
to Zerubbabel: 'Not by might nor by power,
*but by my Spirit,' says the L*ORD *Almighty."*

ZECHARIAH 4:6

MY SPIRIT IS YOUR FUEL FOR LIVING. Depend on My love, wisdom, and grace to get you through each day. When you live dependent on the Spirit, I will lead and guide you, provide comfort and courage, and gently teach and convict you. It's so easy for you to take the reins of your life and live independently. Don't try to control your circumstances and live in your own strength, instead, wait on My power to accomplish My will for you. I understand that releasing control may make you feel anxious, but trust Me and patiently wait for direction. As you come to Me in prayer and thanksgiving, My peace that surpasses all human understanding will flood your heart, mind, and soul. Continually invite My Spirit to fill you, and I will clear the clouds of confusion and bring peace and clarity.

Heavenly Father, deliver me from leaning into my power and lead me to be wholly dependent on Your Spirit. Thank You for offering peace in the midst of whatever I face.

If we confess our sins, He is faithful and righteous,
so that He will forgive us our sins and cleanse
us from all unrighteousness.

1 JOHN 1:9, NASB

YOU ARE FORGIVEN because of My Son's death on the cross. However, unconfessed sin in your life creates a barrier between you and Me. It produces guilt in you, which can cause you to hide or turn away from Me. I sacrificed what is most precious to Me—My Son—to pay your debt of sin. Don't allow sin to come between us. Confess it to Me—I already know about it anyway—and I will wipe your heart clean. My soul cleansing offers freedom and a clear conscience, and all you need to do is ask for it.

Heavenly Father, lead me into repentance to remove any barrier that prevents intimacy with You. I ask for Your mercy and forgiveness. Cleanse me with Your grace and love.

Jesus told his disciples a parable to show
them that they should always pray and not give up.

LUKE 18:1

PRAYER IS LIKE A 24-HOUR HOTLINE TO ME. I am always available for your heartfelt prayers, and I don't reject your requests to Me. Even though you may not think I hear you, I do. You may not always get what you want when you want it because My will may be entirely different from your request. But know that I hear you, and I care. I care so much that at times I must direct you in a way that doesn't make sense to you. My Spirit is always at work in you—I have a plan and see the entire picture and know what is ultimately best for you. Part of My plan is for you to trust Me. When you trust Me, you will experience My faithfulness, which produces more faith in Me. Whatever you do, don't give up coming to Me in prayer. Your part is to pray and show up; the rest is up to Me. No matter what, pray and don't give up!

Heavenly Father, it's hard to believe that You are always available. Thank You for allowing me to come to You with the same requests over and over. Give me faith to trust You even when I don't understand.

FEBRUARY 29

Let us not become weary in doing good, for at the proper time we will reap a harvest if we do not give up.

GALATIANS 6:9

MY SPIRIT STRENGTHENS YOUR WEARY SOUL. Everyone is needy. It's just a matter of time until each person has to learn how to receive from Me. I desire to use you to meet the needs of others through the power of My Spirit. When you work in your own strength, you will become weary and resentful. These will be signs that you are not depending on My Spirit to accomplish My work. When My Spirit is at work through you, you will be able to love like Me. You will have joy and peace that is contagious. You will exercise self-control you didn't realize you have. You will exude patience, kindness, goodness, faithfulness, and gentleness.

Heavenly Father, invigorate me with a fresh dose of Your life-giving Spirit. Use me to accomplish Your will in my life and the lives of others. Remind me to rely on Your Spirit's strength rather than my own.

MARCH

*The Lord is the Spirit,
and where the Spirit of the Lord is,
there is freedom.*

2 CORINTHIANS 3:17

MARCH 1

*Jesus said, "Let the little children come to me,
and do not hinder them, for the kingdom of heaven
belongs to such as these."*

MATTHEW 19:14

I GENTLY LOVE LITTLE CHILDREN and offer them lavish affection, even when it cannot be reciprocated. I offer you unconditional love and acceptance too. My Spirit empowers you to trust Me with childlike faith, know Me as a good Father, and follow Me wherever I lead. My beloved child, My kingdom belongs to you. Trust Me as you walk in My affection.

Heavenly Father, help me to put away my immature, childish ways and grow a humble, childlike faith. Help me to quickly recognize pride in my heart so I can cultivate a heart like Yours.

Be imitators of God, as beloved children;
and walk in love, just as Christ also loved you
and gave Himself up for us, an offering and a
sacrifice to God as a fragrant aroma.

EPHESIANS 5:1–2, NASB

MY LOVE AND GRACE are a gift. Have you begun to comprehend the depth and breadth of My magnificent love for you? I am the lover of your soul! A close friend may give you a cold shoulder, but I will warmly console your concerns and silence your fears. I accept you despite your failures. You can't earn My love—it's a free gift to you. When you or others place expectations of perfection on you, they weigh you down and make you anxious. But My grace is sufficient for you, for My power is made perfect in weakness. Come to Me for comfort, not condemnation.

Heavenly Father, grow my heart of compassion and empower me with the same grace and love You extend to me so I can extend it to all I come in contact with. I want to be a source of comfort rather than a critic.

Peter came to Jesus and asked, "Lord, how many times shall I forgive my brother or sister who sins against me? Up to seven times?" Jesus answered, "I tell you, not seven times, but seventy-seven times."

MATTHEW 18:21–22

MY FORGIVENESS DOES NOT EXPIRE. If someone crushes your dreams, forgive. If someone steals from you, forgive. If you are cheated, forgive. If someone lies to you, forgive. Do you see My pattern? No matter the offense, forgive. Forgive as I forgave you. No sin is too great, too evil, or too personal to be forgiven. Unforgiveness hurts you, My child. It is heavy and weighs you down. It tortures the soul and will make you bitter. If you harbor unforgiveness, you will lose. Follow My example and freely forgive. I want to heal your soul, and the first step is for you to abundantly forgive. Allow the power of the Holy Spirit to work in you to forgive all those who have hurt you. When you follow My example and freely forgive, you will walk in freedom.

Heavenly Father, I am so undeserving of Your ongoing forgiveness, yet You freely bestow it upon me. Help my gratitude translate into forgiving anyone for anything.

MARCH 4

For if you forgive other people when they sin
against you, your heavenly Father will also forgive you.
But if you do not forgive others their sins,
your Father will not forgive your sins.

MATTHEW 6:14–15

SOAK UP THE GIFT OF MY FORGIVENESS, and then give it away to those who have offended you. Unforgiveness will hinder you and will create a wall between you and Me, blocking our intimacy. Unforgiveness is not letting someone off the hook—it will set you free. Invite My Spirit into the dark places of your heart to empower you to forgive fast and often. And forgive thoroughly—an ounce of bitterness or the smallest of grudges will grow and cause spiritual cancer in your heart. I canceled your debt of sin, so why would you want to harbor bitterness, resentment, and unforgiveness toward those who offend you? When you forgive, you trust Me to judge others in My time. My judgment is just. Your hurting heart can be healed by forgiveness and love.

Heavenly Father, I want nothing to hinder my rela-
tionship with You. Grant me a heart of forgiveness to
forgive like You. I trust You to be the final judge.

When you ask, you must believe and not doubt, because the one who doubts is like a wave of the sea, blown and tossed by the wind. That person should not expect to receive anything from the Lord. Such a person is double-minded and unstable in all they do.

JAMES 1:6–8

DOUBLE-MINDEDNESS COMES FROM DOUBT, not from the Spirit. Doubt about your career. Doubt about your finances. Doubt about your relationships. Doubt about Me. When doubt and confusion creep in, your faith and hope waver and cause instability and insecurity. Have doubt and double-mindedness frozen your faith? Create space in your heart for My Spirit to strengthen your faith as you learn to listen for My quiet voice. My Spirit clarifies and confirms My will for you. As you exercise your faith, the Spirit will melt away your fears, strengthen your faith, and bring stability.

Heavenly Father, I bring my doubts to You and look to You for clarification and reassurance. I don't want to be blown and tossed by the wind—You are my firm foundation. Help my faith to daily grow in You.

God is not a God of confusion but of peace.

1 CORINTHIANS 14:33, ESV

WHEN YOUR LIFE FEELS OUT OF CONTROL, I will bring order to your chaos. When you feel confused, divided, or torn, it's time to slip away to a quiet place with Me and allow My Spirit to usher in orderliness and peace. I designed the universe with purpose and intent; confusion is a signal for you to slow down and wait on Me. I will help you navigate any situation you encounter. The key is to adjust as the Spirit directs you. It will become easier with time and practice. When you let go and trust Me, My Spirit will cover you with peace and bring clarity.

Heavenly Father, thank You that chaos and confusion are signals for me to draw near to You and ask for help. Give me a clear mind and peace in my spirit so I can discern Your will.

Jesus replied: "'Love the Lord your God with all your heart and with all your soul and with all your mind."

MATTHEW 22:37

LOVE ME WITH ALL OF YOUR HEART. I want you to know Me in such a way that you develop a heart of gratitude for My grace, a heart of joy for My friendship, and a heart of hope for My heavenly home. Fix your eyes on eternity rather than exclusively focusing on the world in which you live. Worry will wreck your life, especially when your heart is consumed with what you can't control. Trust Me with your whole heart. Love Me vulnerably. Above all else, guard your heart with My love and know that you are Mine.

Heavenly Father, fill my cup to overflowing with Your love, for when I am anchored in Your love I am stripped of worry, anxiety, and the pull of this world. Help me to be a beacon of Your love in a world that is consumed with looking for love in all the wrong places.

Do not conform to the pattern of this world, but be transformed by the renewing of your mind. Then you will be able to test and approve what God's will is—his good, pleasing and perfect will.

ROMANS 12:2

I WANT TO TRANSFORM YOU from the inside out and make you a reflection of Me. Spending time with Me changes how you think so that you can begin to understand My will for your life. My will is not elusive, but attainable to you. As you earnestly seek Me, the Spirit will help you discern My Word and My ways. You will learn how to test and approve My will so that your faith and character grow and My best for you becomes clear. As you submit your mind to the transforming power of the Spirit, you will gain clarity and confidence to mature in your faith and become more like Me.

Heavenly Father, change me from the inside out. Make me more like You each and every day. Renew my mind with Your transforming Spirit of understanding and wisdom.

Be kind and compassionate to one another,
forgiving each other, just as in Christ God forgave you.

EPHESIANS 4:32

YOU ARE FULLY AND COMPLETELY FORGIVEN, which enables you to wholly forgive. Your ability to forgive flows from the flood of My forgiveness. Forgiven people forgive out of eternal gratitude for My grace and forgiveness. My mercy and compassion empower you to forgive; without it, you will suffer in a cycle of unforgiveness—tormented by hurt—and grow bitter. Unforgiveness can make you physically ill, My child. The Spirit will set you free from the bondage of unforgiveness and clear the path for you to continually forgive others.

Heavenly Father, help me to consciously and consistently walk in the freedom You paid such a dear price for me to experience. Break any cycles of unforgiveness in my life, and expand my ability to forgive as a reflection of how You have forgiven me.

Anyone you forgive, I also forgive. And what I have forgiven—if there was anything to forgive—I have forgiven in the sight of Christ for your sake, in order that Satan might not outwit us. For we are not unaware of his schemes.

2 CORINTHIANS 2:10–11

FORGIVENESS IS THE KEY to intimacy with Me. Unforgiveness eats away at intimacy with Me, your family, and your friends. Without forgiveness, you will lash out at those you love. My love and kindness tear down walls, and My grace and forgiveness build bridges of hope. Your intimacy with Me grows deeper as you freely forgive. Invite My Spirit to search your heart and reveal any unforgiveness you are suppressing and concealing. The Enemy wants to sabotage your relationships and isolate you. Refuse to let the Enemy outwit you. Rather, continually forgive as I continually forgive you. You'll find it's a much easier load to carry.

Heavenly Father, prevent the Enemy from blinding me to the freedom of forgiveness and deceiving me into believing I have a right to hold a grudge, remain bitter, or harbor unforgiveness. Thank You for paving the way to forgive on the cross. Empower me to wholly forgive and release the heavy burden of unforgiveness.

MARCH 11

You will keep in perfect peace those whose minds are
steadfast, because they trust in you. Trust in the LORD
forever, for the LORD, the LORD himself, is the Rock eternal.

ISAIAH 26:3–4

MY PEACE IS PERFECT AND PERMANENT. Beware of the world's imperfect, temporary peace that masks itself in the form of materialism, relationships, a career, a pill, or a bottle. Artificial peace restricts and rejects Me, the Prince of Peace. Counterfeit peace prolongs pain and leads to long-term disappointment and disillusionment. My Spirit produces peace that guards your heart and mind from incessant worry and fear of the unknown when you set your thoughts on Me. Open the door to My perfect peace by wholly trusting Me, your Rock. I am with you always.

Heavenly Father, I am forever grateful for Your peace
that calms my heart and settles my mind. Renew my
heart and mind with the truth of Your Word when I
begin to drown in hopelessness and anxiety. Help me
to plant my feet on Your firm foundation, my Rock and
Redeemer.

I baptize you with water for repentance.
But after me comes one who is more powerful than I,
whose sandals I am not worthy to carry. He will
baptize you with the Holy Spirit and fire.

MATTHEW 3:11

WHEN YOU PLACE YOUR FAITH IN ME, I deposit the Holy Spirit in you. My Spirit is a gift to help you grow. He infuses you with faith and power to live the new life to which I have called you. The Spirit empowers you to walk in newness of life as My child. Spending time with Me is the best way to learn how to hear Me. The longer you walk with Me, the easier it will be to recognize the still, quiet promptings of the Spirit in your heart. However, if you begin to silence the Spirit, it will be difficult to detect what He is saying to you. I caution you not to neglect the Spirit. He will never leave you, but learning to listen and discern His voice takes time. The Holy Spirit is your helper and only wants what is best for you.

Spirit of God, forgive me when I ignore or silence You. Help me to respond swiftly to You so I don't become dull to Your promptings. Teach me to have the mind of Christ and walk in step with You.

I have listened to the voice of the LORD my God;
I have acted in accordance with everything that
You have commanded me.

DEUTERONOMY 26:14, NASB

LISTEN TO MY VOICE in the silence of meditating on My Word. Our time together is like a map to show you how to follow Me. I remind you of how delighted I am with your heart to follow Me. Your desire to love as I love, to forgive as I forgive, and to serve as I serve is pleasing to Me. My Spirit enables you to imitate Me. He fills and empowers you to do all I ask you to do.

Heavenly Father, I listen to Your voice as I mediate on Your Word. Help me to walk in obedience as I follow wherever You lead.

Since we live by the Spirit,
let us keep in step with the Spirit.

GALATIANS 5:25

I CAN SEE CLEARLY WHAT AWAITS YOU. Stay in step with the Spirit and trust Me to be the eyes of your soul. Circumstances may appear cloudy, but I am able to lift the clouds and move you from confusion to clarity and confidence. I am your salvation—the Shepherd of your soul. I know what the future holds, and although I don't always reveal it to you, I am trustworthy. When you trust Me with the unknown, your faith will flourish as you wait on Me to work. Rely on the Spirit to guide you one step at a time.

Heavenly Father, I am so grateful that You are all-knowing and in control. Help me to stop trying to control and plan every aspect of my life, but to instead trust You as my Shepherd. I don't need to know the future when I know the One who holds my future.

Jesus, full of the Holy Spirit, left the Jordan and was led by the Spirit into the wilderness.

LUKE 4:1

FEAR NOT when you find yourself in the wilderness. There will be seasons when My Spirit leads you into wilderness experiences, even a spiritual desert. In Me, you have everything you need to persevere. Empty yourself of all expectations and replace them with the promise that I will never leave or forsake you. In this desolate and lonely land, I will mold you and teach you to recognize My voice more clearly and show you who you are in Me. The Spirit will sustain your strength and guide you through the wilderness, and nothing will be wasted.

Spirit of God, by faith I release my expectations and trust that what You desire for me is best. Help me to cling to You rather than grasp at the temporary fixes of this world.

No temptation has overtaken you except what is common to mankind. And God is faithful; he will not let you be tempted beyond what you can bear. But when you are tempted, he will also provide a way out so that you can endure it.

1 CORINTHIANS 10:13

I AM FULLY AWARE OF EVERY TEMPTATION you will encounter today. There is no temptation you will face that I haven't also faced, and I have made a way of escape for you in every single temptation through the power of the Spirit. He strengthens and enables you to withstand any temptation. This is the same Spirit—the Holy Spirit—who strengthened Jesus when He was tempted in the wilderness. Just as Jesus used Scripture to stand against temptation, the Spirit will illuminate My Word to give you discernment and understanding. Come against the Enemy with Scripture to defeat his foolish and unseemly ways. My Spirit and My Word empower you to consistently overcome and defeat temptation.

Spirit of God, show me the truth of Scripture and empower me to overcome any temptation I face today and always.

Do not be foolish, but understand what the Lord's will is. Do not get drunk on wine, which leads to debauchery. Instead, be filled with the Spirit.

EPHESIANS 5:17–18

ALLOW MY SPIRIT TO HAVE CONTROL OF YOU. This is quite the opposite of *losing* control; it's *giving* Me control. The fear of losing control is simply an illusion, My child, because you've never really had control. Rather, I am in control—yesterday, today, and tomorrow—and I've never, not even for a moment, lost control. When your world seems to spin out of control, I am holding all things together and working them for the good of My children. When you surrender to the Spirit's control, you will experience My peace—a peace that won't make sense to onlookers who don't know Me. When you are filled with the Spirit, He will produce love, joy, peace, patience, kindness, goodness, faithfulness, gentleness, and self-control in you.

Spirit of God, I recognize that I am not—and never have been—in control. I joyfully give You complete control and ask You to fill me. May Your wisdom and power be the controlling influence in my life.

MARCH 18

*Jesus returned to Galilee in the power of the Spirit,
and news about him spread through the whole countryside.
He was teaching in their synagogues,
and everyone praised him.*

LUKE 4:14–15

I WANT YOU TO SUCCEED, but the success I want for you comes from dependence on the Spirit's power in your life. If the approval of people is your test for success, you will live in a perpetual state of anxious uncertainty. I am at work in you, with you, and through you by the power of the Spirit. Trust Me for success and you will experience purpose and fulfillment regardless of the outcome. My idea of success is far more about *who* you are than *what* you do. The work of the Spirit quietly invades your heart and brings glory to Me for your success.

Heavenly Father, forgive me for looking for the applause and acceptance of people. You are the only One I want to please. Constantly remind me to rest in You and allow Your Spirit to accomplish Your will through me. I pray that my approval and success will rest in the affirmation of Your Spirit.

Be strong and courageous. Do not be afraid or terrified because of them, for the LORD your God goes with you; he will never leave you nor forsake you.

DEUTERONOMY 31:6

I SEE YOU and the world in which you live. There are countless reasons for you to live in constant fear. Sickness, death, and natural disasters surround you on a daily basis. At times, life appears unfair and unkind. I am aware of every detail of your life, and I offer hope. When life isn't easy and your struggles appear to be more than you can handle, rely on My Spirit for the strength you need. Once on the other side, you will be able to look back and see the ways in which I carried you and cared for you. I will never leave you, and I will never fail you. The Spirit supplies strength when you are tired, hurting, and weak. I supply all of your needs. As you train your eyes and ears to focus on Me, you learn to walk by faith rather than fear.

Heavenly Father, forgive me for so often walking in fear and doubt. Thank You for carrying me when I can't stand on my own. I place my faith in You and trust You with all of my life.

*Now this is our boast: Our conscience testifies
that we have conducted ourselves in the world,
and especially in our relations with you, with integrity
and godly sincerity. We have done so, relying not
on worldly wisdom but on God's grace.*

2 CORINTHIANS 1:12

YOU CAN RELY ON ME FOR WISDOM. When you don't know what to do, which way to go, or how to determine which path to choose, seek Me and My wisdom. I will generously give it to those who ask Me. It's tempting to rely on what seemed to work in the past or what works for someone else instead of relying on Me for wisdom. You are constantly bombarded with information—don't confuse knowledge with true wisdom. Worldly wisdom has a way of reducing My wisdom to an afterthought. Seek Me, My Word, and the counsel of those who are wise in My ways. My Spirit is ready and willing to pour out My abundant wisdom on you.

Heavenly Father, give me discernment to know the difference between worldly wisdom and Your wisdom. Remind me to seek Your Word and grant me clarity in discerning Your voice.

It seems foolish to the Jews because they want a sign from heaven as proof that what is preached is true; and it is foolish to the Gentiles because they believe only what agrees with their philosophy and seems wise to them. . . .
But God has opened the eyes of those called to salvation.

1 CORINTHIANS 1:22, 24, TLB

I AM FULL OF POWER AND WISDOM, which My Son demonstrated during His life on earth—yet so many missed who He was. It is no different today; many require signs and wonders or intellectual evidence, missing the fact that I humbled Myself and entered your world in all My deity in the form of Jesus. Ask Me who I am, and the Spirit will reveal Me to you; He is the source of wise counsel. Don't get caught up in looking for signs or seeking miracles to test if you are hearing My voice. Learn to hear the Spirit's still, quiet whisper. Access wisdom from My Word and power from the Spirit. The Spirit opens your eyes to see Me and your ears to hear Me.

Heavenly Father, help me to catch myself when I'm looking for a sign to prove You are at work in my life. Your Word is all I need to know that You are with me always and freely offer Your wisdom.

My God will supply all your needs according
to His riches in glory in Christ Jesus.

PHILIPPIANS 4:19, NASB

I AM YOUR PROVIDER. My heart's desire is to provide for you, and it will often come in the least likely ways. Generosity is My very nature, and it gives Me great pleasure to provide for you. When you fear, I provide peace. When you are lonely, I provide companionship. When you suffer, I provide comfort. When you lack necessities, I provide for your needs. When you are insecure, I provide inner strength and confidence. Just as an earthly father delights in providing for his children, so I delight in being your provider.

Heavenly Father, help me not to miss all the ways You provide for me. I am so often deceived by self-reliance and believe I provide for myself. Thank You for providing for me materially, physically, and spiritually.

MARCH 23

*The L*ORD *is good, a refuge in times of trouble.*
He cares for those who trust in him.

NAHUM 1:7

I AM GOOD. I am good during your best days and your worst days. I am good when you experience difficult and painful circumstances. I am good when you are in the midst of crisis, suffering in sickness, or mourning the loss of a loved one. I am always good. My goodness is a refuge for you in times of trouble. My Spirit unleashes goodness and offers security, for I will always act in accordance with what is right, true, and good. Rest in My goodness when you are exhausted and weak, and My Spirit will strengthen you. Trust My goodness, and allow Me to be your refuge.

Heavenly Father, saturate me in Your goodness all the days of my life. Renew my mind when I question Your goodness because of my circumstances. You are my refuge and strength.

*Abraham believed God, and it was credited to him as
righteousness, and he was called God's friend.*

JAMES 2:23

WHEN YOU PLACED YOUR FAITH IN ME, I redeemed
you and became your friend. As with all relationships,
our love will continue to grow and flourish as we spend
time together. Ask the Spirit to lead you into a deeper
understanding of Me. Seek Me for advice, and I will teach
you My wise ways, which are always best for you. You can
know Me as a friend and trust Me as your Father. I am
with you. I am for you. Always.

*Heavenly Father, thank You for the privilege of calling
You friend. Give me a deep desire to spend time with
You and develop an intimate friendship with You.*

When they [Paul and Barnabas] came to Jerusalem, they were welcomed by the church and the apostles and elders, to whom they reported everything God had done through them.

ACTS 15:4

MY WORK IN YOUR LIFE is personal but not private. Be confident and bold to tell others about what I am doing in and through you. Encourage those around you to trust Me as you have trusted Me. My provision is for all who place their faith in Me. The Spirit will guide you as you humbly and gratefully share what I am doing in your life, and He will stir others to seek Me through your testimony.

Spirit of God, give me the courage to declare who You are to those who don't know You and strengthen my faith as I watch You transform others as You've transformed me.

For we live by faith, not by sight.

2 CORINTHIANS 5:7

I HAVE A VISION FOR YOUR LIFE. I desire you to live a life of faith focused on Me. You will not immediately see everything I have for you in the future, but as we journey together, trust Me to reveal to you what you need when you need it. Learn to trust and follow the Spirit, especially when it feels uncomfortable and uncertain. I will surprise and delight you as you learn to live by faith rather than sight. I deeply desire an intimate relationship with you. Explore My possibilities by looking around you with eyes of faith and eager anticipation of My plan for your life.

Heavenly Father, expand my view of You and all You have for my life. Help me to recognize Your love and rest in Your will for me.

After leaving them, [Jesus] went up
on a mountainside to pray.

MARK 6:46

PRAYER IS A TIME FOR ME TO SETTLE YOUR SOUL with My calming Spirit and an opportunity for you to grow in understanding of My deep, unconditional love for you. I eagerly anticipate our time together, My precious child. As you disconnect from the distractions in your life and connect with Me, the Spirit fills your heart with My peaceful presence. The world you live in applauds busyness and activity, but the Spirit energizes you and instructs your mind in stillness and waiting. Prayer is where I do My best work of caring for your soul, bearing your burdens, and extinguishing burnout.

Heavenly Father, help me to slow down and listen to You. I want to pray in stillness, but I also want to pray when I am on the move. Most of all, I want to know You better.

MARCH 28

So God led the people around by the
desert road toward the Red Sea.

EXODUS 13:18

TRUST ME TO LEAD YOU. My path for you may include a desert or a valley before you enter My promised land. The wilderness is where I will uncover your deepest desires and align them with My heart and desires for you. Uncertainty will try to rob you of your joy; instead, you can lean into My unfailing and unchanging love for you. My Spirit always dwells within you and sustains you. Even when you don't feel His presence, He is with you. The desert is where I will do heart surgery to rid you of self-righteous pride and replace it with selfless humility. Trust Me. I know the way. I *am* the way.

Spirit of the Lord, lead me along the path less traveled and mold me into Your image. Give me faith to follow You through deserts and valleys, and help me to savor Your power, love, and grace on the mountaintops.

*When his master saw that the L*ORD *was with him and that
the L*ORD *gave him success in everything he did, Joseph
found favor in his eyes and became his attendant.*

GENESIS 39:3–4

RELY ON MY SPIRIT TO GUIDE YOU in what to do. Do
your work for Me, and others will recognize that I am
with you. Even when you find yourself in unfavorable
positions, My hand will be on you. My Spirit will empower you to give life to others. Even unbelievers will know
something is different about you. Remain a faithful leader
at home and work, and you will earn the trust of people
who need to trust Me. Success comes *from* Me and *for*
Me. Trust Me to use you in all circumstances.

*Spirit of God, empower me to be an example of Your
grace at home and work. May any success I have be a
reflection of You.*

I waited patiently for the LORD;
he turned to me and heard my cry.

PSALM 40:1

PATIENTLY WAIT ON ME FOR MY BEST. Those who are patient—those who wait—will receive My greatest gifts. Patience is a fruit of the Spirit, but also a vehicle in which I deliver My blessings. While you wait, pray fervently and rest in My abundant love. I hear your cry and have not forgotten you. Fear not, for I am faithful and trustworthy and give you the Spirit to uphold you.

Heavenly Father, You are so patient with me. Give me strength to wait on You and a patient heart like Yours to extend patience to those I meet every day.

MARCH 31

*You, however, are not in the realm of the flesh but are
in the realm of the Spirit, if indeed the Spirit of God lives
in you. And if anyone does not have the Spirit of Christ,
they do not belong to Christ.*

ROMANS 8:9

YOU BELONG TO ME, and My Spirit lives in you. The Spirit is like a superpower for you. He's not magic—you simply have to let go and allow Him to guide you. When you are unsure, the Spirit gives wisdom. When you struggle with fear and anxiety, the Spirit ushers in peace. When you begin to drift and are tempted to follow your own way, the Spirit will lead you into My will. I gave you the Spirit to comfort you, intercede for you, and advocate for you. Allow the Spirit to empower you daily to walk in the freedom I provided through Christ.

Spirit of God, I praise and thank You that You live in me and empower me to walk in freedom. Prompt me throughout my day to tune my ear to Your voice and let You lead me.

APRIL

Those who are led by the Spirit of
God are the children of God.

ROMANS 8:14

Set your affection on things above,
not on things on the earth.

COLOSSIANS 3:2, KJV

I DESIRE ALL OF YOUR AFFECTION. There are so many idols in this world competing for your affection. The idol of lust discredits your integrity. The idol of work robs your relationships. The idol of money enslaves you to work. Distorted love leaves you longing for My perfect love. My love satisfies your deepest needs. Acceptance, attention, and approval all flow freely from My heart. I am all you need. Devote yourself to Me and allow My Spirit to excavate your heart of idols. When you set your affections on Me, I will usher in peace and hope and offer a life of rest rather than a life of struggle and exhaustion.

Heavenly Father, draw my heart into the deep affections of Your perfect love. Help me to rest in You and focus on what's most important to You. You are all I need.

APRIL 2

If any of you lacks wisdom, you should ask God,
who gives generously.

JAMES 1:5

I WANT TO GENEROUSLY GIVE YOU MY WISDOM.
There is no question or problem you can't bring to Me.
Don't be afraid to ask Me tough questions—I have a
never-ending supply of patience and understanding. You
simply need to ask Me. Make your pursuit of My wisdom
a lifelong aim. Pursue your dreams, but first pursue My
wisdom. Trust Me alone. I am honored and exalted when
you seek My wisdom, counsel, and direction for your life.
Ask Me—I'm waiting to generously shower you with My
wisdom.

Heavenly Father, I seek Your wisdom to live my life ac-
cording to Your plan and principles. Draw me back to
Your wisdom when I begin to seek answers apart from
You. Thank You for generously giving Your wisdom.

APRIL 3

I am the living bread that came down from heaven. Whoever eats this bread will live forever. This bread is my flesh, which I will give for the life of the world.

JOHN 6:51

ONLY I CAN SATISFY YOUR HUNGRY SOUL. I am the Bread of Life. Feast on Me, and My peace will free your heart from the burdens and pain of this world. Just as you require daily food to sustain your physical body, so it is with Me. Eat the bread of My truth each day, and your mind will be renewed, refreshed, and nourished with wisdom. Your soul will wither if it lacks My nourishment. Take of My daily bread in prayer and solitude to fuel your heart, mind, and soul, and ask the Spirit to fill you to overflowing with My presence.

Heavenly Father, You are life. Nourish me each day with Your truth, love, and peace. May Your Spirit empower me to surrender to You moment by moment.

Who shall separate us from the love of Christ?

ROMANS 8:35

NOTHING WILL SEPARATE YOU FROM MY LOVE. No tragedy, no hardship, no loss will separate you from My love. My love is permanent and a comfort to your heart and soul. When you feel separated from relationships with those you love, allow the Spirit to draw you to Me. My love shows up for you when others can't. My love speaks up for you when others won't. My love provides for you when others are unable. My love is unconditional and unfailing, infinite and pure. And My love is always accessible to you. Nothing can separate you from My love. Rest in My everlasting love and unfailing kindness.

Heavenly Father, I am overwhelmed by Your love. I don't have to earn it, and I can't lose it. Thank You for Your assurance that nothing can separate me from Your great love that never fails and is always accessible.

APRIL 5

Whoever lives by the truth comes into the light,
so that it may be seen plainly that what they
have done has been done in the sight of God.

JOHN 3:21

I AM THE TRUTH, and there is no darkness in Me. Walk in My light, free from fear and condemnation. I did not send My Son—the Light of the World—into the world to condemn you, but to save you. Evil lurks in the darkness, producing fear and crippling your faith. As you walk with the Spirit in the light of My love and truth, you will experience freedom and peace. When you walk in light, there is nothing to hide. Satan flees at the sight of My light and the sound of My Word. Call upon the Spirit to lead you away from the shadows and into the truth of My light.

Heavenly Father, thank You for sending the Light of the World to save me. I want to walk by faith in the light and truth of Your Word to experience fullness of life in You.

He heals the brokenhearted and binds up their wounds.

PSALM 147:3

I VALUE YOU as My precious child. As a mother nurtures her child with love and compassion, so I care for your heart. I know the deep recesses of your heart where darkness, pain, and sin reside. Your motives are not hidden from Me. Come to Me just as you are and allow the Spirit to shine My light in the secret places of your soul. I am humble and gentle and will lovingly guide you out of darkness and into truth. I will heal your wounds and help you walk into newness of life in Me. I invite you into the secret place of intimate communion with Me. Rest in My unconditional love and acceptance.

Heavenly Father, thank You for loving me as I am and for gently leading me out of the darkness of the world and into Your life-giving ways. I don't want to justify my actions and make excuses. I want to live in Your truth and freedom and be pleasing in Your sight.

God is so rich in mercy and loves
us with such intense love.

EPHESIANS 2:4, CJB

I LIFT YOU OUT OF YOUR PAIN AND REGRET and shower you with My forgiveness and unconditional love. Don't allow guilt and shame to weigh you down, keep you in your pit of pain, and create distance between us. Past decisions do not define you. My forgiveness defines you and claims you as My beloved child. The pain I suffered on the cross heals your pain of sin and sorrow. My Spirit immerses you in My amazing grace and liberating truth. I wipe your slate clean and make you white as snow. Come home to My extravagant love, where My overflowing joy is freely available to you.

Heavenly Father, Your love is extravagant. I choose to cling to Your mercy and forgiveness instead of my sin and shame. You are all I need to become everything You want me to be.

We love because he first loved us.

1 JOHN 4:19

I INITIATED LOVE FOR YOU FIRST. The Spirit enables you to love Me, love yourself, and love others. Your capacity to love is only limited by your willingness to allow My love to flow through you. I desire for you to grow in grace and love—becoming fluent in patience, kindness, joy, forgiveness, selflessness, gratitude, and generosity. These are the ways you demonstrate My love. And just as you can't out-give Me, you can't out-love Me. My love is like an ocean—vast and deep and boundless. It is refreshing and will never run dry. As you soak in My love, it will spill onto to those around you.

Heavenly Father, You love me even when I am unlovable. Grow my capacity to be loved by You so I can grow in capacity to love You and others.

We are God's handiwork,
created in Christ Jesus to do good works,
which God prepared in advance for us to do.

EPHESIANS 2:10

MY STRENGTH IS SUFFICIENT FOR YOU to serve others. My Spirit will fuel you to serve in My name. Service is a sacred experience allowing you to be used by Me to accomplish My plans for you and others. Remain prayerful and faithful. Serving in your own strength leads to exhaustion and burnout. Serving by the power of My Spirit is exhilarating and energizing. Your faith will be an adventure, void of boredom, when you allow the Spirit to lead you.

Heavenly Father, I surrender my heart to Your strength so that I can live a life of service to You. It is an honor and privilege to be used by You. Help me to remain humble and allow You to work in and through me.

Be devoted to one another in love.
Honor one another above yourselves.

ROMANS 12:10

YOU HONOR ME when you love and honor others, even when they aren't lovable or behaving honorably. The Holy Spirit empowers you to model My devotion by being devoted to, caring and providing for, and unconditionally loving others. Honor speaks words that lift and build up. Honor is exemplified when you pursue hard-to-love people. Love rises above feelings of disrespect and takes the high road of honor. My Spirit propels you to honor others above yourself just as I love and honor you.

Spirit of God, I am incapable of loving and honoring others on my own. Empower me to love and honor those who are difficult to respect in the same way You shower me with Your unmerited mercy, grace, and love.

*Then he said to them, "Watch out! Be on your
guard against all kinds of greed; life does not consist
in an abundance of possessions."*

LUKE 12:15

EXCESSIVE MATERIAL POSSESSIONS WILL DISTRACT
rather than satisfy you. Let My Spirit create a contentedness in you—a deep, spiritual richness. Build My kingdom, not a kingdom of this world. My life in you is great
gain. You will experience a truly rich life by knowing Me,
making Me known, loving others, and giving your life
away. You will find peace and rest as you learn to be content in Me.

*Heavenly Father, help me to loosen my grip on the
things of this world and live with open hands and an
open heart. Give me a spirit of contentedness and generosity to love and serve others by the power of Your
Spirit.*

Whoever wants to save their life will lose it,
but whoever loses their life for me will find it.

MATTHEW 16:25

I OFFER YOU THE GREAT EXCHANGE. If you lose your life for My sake, you will find true life. Lose your life and surrender to Me to discover My will for you. My Son laid down His life to save yours, and My Spirit enables you to die to yourself. When you lay your life down for others in My name, you will point them to Me and the free gift of life I offer. Your life is temporary—a quickly vanishing vapor. I am storing up for you eternal riches that far outweigh any cost in your present life. I am life.

Jesus, thank You for giving Your life for me and raising me up to live for You. Give me the strength and courage to die to my old way of life and take up real life in You.

Greater love has no one than this: to lay down one's life for one's friends. You are my friends if you do what I command.

JOHN 15:13–14

LOVE IS MY MOTIVATION for being in a relationship with you. Because of My great love for you, I laid down My son's life for you. I want you to know deep in your soul how special you are to Me. We are forever friends, even when circumstances create distance between us. Your faith in Me will expand your heart and grow your intimacy with Me. You can completely trust Me to do what is best for you. The Spirit will make Me known to you as you walk with Me into the unknown. I love you with an infinite and boundless love.

Heavenly Father, thank You for loving me so much that You gave Your Son's life for me; there truly is no greater love. Help me to never forget what a privilege it is to be called Your friend. Give me the courage to walk in Your ways today and to trust You today and every day.

*For though the righteous fall seven times, they rise again,
but the wicked stumble when calamity strikes.*

PROVERBS 24:16

MY MERCY PICKS YOU UP when you fall down. I am proud of you for moving out of your comfort zone and trying new things. If you never fall, you will fail to stretch your faith for My sake. I define success by the motives of your heart. Each time you fall, it's simply a stepping-stone on a path to faithfully following Me. As you learn to follow Me, the Holy Spirit refines humility in you, strengthens your steadfastness in Me, and expands what you think is possible even when it feels uncomfortable or scary. He will raise you up, allowing you to stand firm in Me and strengthening your faith.

Heavenly Father, lift me up by the power of Your Spirit when I stumble and fall. Thank You for not expecting perfection from me, but instead using my failures and mistakes as opportunities to trust You more and strengthen my faith.

Every word of God is flawless;
he is a shield to those who take refuge in him.

PROVERBS 30:5

MY WORDS ARE TRUE and will reassure you. Hear My heart for you: I love you more than your mind can grasp. I am here for you. I am with you no matter what may come your way. I adore you and approve of you. I uniquely created you—there is no one like you. You are beautiful. You are My beloved. My Spirit dwells in you and is a source of revelation, wisdom, and power for you. Hide My Word deep within the recesses of your heart and soul like a precious treasure as a reminder that you are Mine. Nothing and no one can snatch you out of My loving hand.

Heavenly Father, help me to know You. Reveal Your thoughts to me. Open my eyes to my identity in Christ and the hope and inheritance that are mine.

My dear brothers and sisters, take note of this:
Everyone should be quick to listen,
slow to speak and slow to become angry.

JAMES 1:19

ALLOW ME TO SPEAK FOR YOU. My wisdom will have you remain quiet at times, especially in the face of unfair criticism. I always bring to light the truth in My timing. I fight spiritual battles unseen by human eyes—only those with eyes of faith can see Me at work. My work in your life will become more evident over time. The Holy Spirit will empower you to patiently wait on Me in silence. I love you, and I see you. I am your shield and defender.

Heavenly Father, I pray for those who misunderstand me to know my true heart. Help me to love the unlovable and those who hurt me. Please give me strength to remain silent and wait on You.

Let the one who is wise heed these things
and ponder the loving deeds of the LORD.

PSALM 107:43, NLT

I AM GOOD, and My love for you endures forever. As you trust Me and rest in My love, you will also grow in wisdom. When your heart overflows with My love, it is humble and open to learning My ways. My Spirit refreshes you and instructs you in My truth and helps you walk in wisdom. Saturate yourself in My abundant love. Humbly follow Me in response to My unfailing love for you.

Heavenly Father, fill my heart to overflowing with Your love and open my mind to Your wisdom.

Jesus wept. Then the Jews said,
"See how he loved him!"

JOHN 11:35–36

ALLOW GRIEF TO LEAD YOU TO ME when you suffer loss. You will be tempted to run from Me during a season of loss, but I am well acquainted with grief, and I hurt with you. My Spirit is your Comforter and consoles you during mourning. He specializes in communicating compassion, care, and comfort, inviting you out of isolation and into intimacy with Me. Bring Me your pain and sorrow in exchange for My peace and comfort.

Heavenly Father, teach me to run to You for love and care during times of loss and pain. You are my comfort. I praise You for Your compassion and mercy.

Anxiety weighs down the heart,
but a kind word cheers it up.

PROVERBS 12:25

I WILL HANDLE WHAT WORRIES YOU and is out of your control. Worry and anxiety will cause spiritual, emotional, and physical ailments for you. Ask the Spirit to usher in My peace and love, to lift the burden of your anxious heart and replace your fear with My hope. Exchange your stressful striving for My patient love. Substitute your worst-case thinking for My truth. Reflect on My steadfast love and faithfulness. Conversation with Me is your time-tested prescription for worry. I will energize your weary soul as you trust Me. I've got this. I've got you.

Heavenly Father, calm my anxious spirit. Teach me to exchange my anxiety and fear for Your peace and love.

My heart, O God, is steadfast;
I will sing and make music with all my soul.

PSALM 108:1

I AM DEPENDABLE AND UNCHANGING, a secure rock upon which you can anchor your heart and life. When you struggle during the storms of life, remember that the storm is temporary, but I am eternal. My Spirit offers peace to soothe you, comfort to help you overcome any difficulty you may face, and strength and hope to ease your trouble and grief. Call upon My loving presence with your song of praise and make music to Me with all your soul. My joy will overflow from your heart, and I will be your strength.

Heavenly Father, help me to anchor my life in Your love. Teach me to sing praise and make music to You rather than flounder in fear. I praise You for Your un-wavering love.

"For my thoughts are not your thoughts, neither are your ways my ways," declares the Lord. "As the heavens are higher than the earth, so are my ways higher than your ways and my thoughts than your thoughts."

ISAIAH 55:8–9

SOMETIMES IT APPEARS that what I ask of you doesn't make sense. When you obey Me even when you don't understand, you'll often find that My plan begins to make sense much later when you look back. Love is My guiding force. My love can be trusted even when your love is tested. My Spirit enables you to persevere when you are willing to trust and obey Me even when you are unsure.

Heavenly Father, give me courage to follow You no matter what. Help me to trust You even when it doesn't make sense in spite of the way I feel.

One who is gracious to a poor person lends to the LORD,
And He will repay him for his good deed.

PROVERBS 19:17, NASB

MY HEART FOR YOU IS TO HEAL the brokenhearted, bandage the wounds of the afflicted, and share the good news of My gospel. I gladly go the extra mile to care for you, and I desire for you to joyfully go above and beyond to care for the hurting. As I am always aware of your needs, look around you for those who need a kind word, a shoulder to cry on, or a generous gift. My definition of greatness is having a big heart to serve others. Slow down and allow the Spirit to direct you to those who are hurting and in need. Serve them in My name by the power of the Spirit and watch Me meet their needs just as I meet yours.

Heavenly Father, open My eyes to people You place around me. Give me an attentive spirit to see the needs of others and the courage to love and serve them in Your name.

*Where two or three gather in my name,
there am I with them.*

MATTHEW 18:20

I AM IN YOUR PRESENCE when you gather with others in My name. Ask My Spirit to lead you to an authentic community of believers. I reveal the power of My love and presence when you gather with other believers unified by My Spirit. The united love of a community of My followers will be a display for all to see My grace at work. Find My followers and gather together in My name.

Heavenly Father, I pray that Your powerful presence will be on display in my life every day, but especially when two or three of us gather in Your name. I yearn to live in Your presence.

They will have no fear of bad news;
their hearts are steadfast, trusting in the LORD.

PSALM 112:7

I AM A FIRM FOUNDATION on which you can stand. When fear of bad news assaults your heart, remain steadfast in your faith as you trust Me. My Spirit will wash over you and help you rest in My presence. My peace is your security. You will remain unshaken and resolute when you wholeheartedly trust Me. Fear tries to seduce you into believing the lie that I am undependable and detached, but the truth is I am always with you and available to you. I invite you to dwell in My shelter and abide in My shadow. I am your refuge and your fortress—you can trust in Me.

Heavenly Father, when I rest in You, it's so much easier to stand firm in my faith. Help me to keep my eyes on You no matter what life brings. Thank You that I am Your beloved and have nothing to fear.

*Those who are led by the Spirit of God
are the children of God.*

ROMANS 8:14

YOU ARE NEVER ALONE. My Spirit leads you, and you are never by yourself. You are My child and are assured the inheritance of eternal life with Me. Your inheritance not only guarantees that you will live forever with Me, it also offers an abundant life on earth for you—a life of love, joy, peace, patience, kindness, goodness, faithfulness, gentleness, self-control. When you follow the Spirit's leading, you demonstrate your spiritual legacy. My Spirit leads you to truth and reveals My deep love for you.

Heavenly Father, thank You for the gift of eternal life with You. When I focus on life with You, everything else pales in comparison. Grow me into Your image so I look more like You and less like the old me.

Love your enemies and pray for those who persecute you,
that you may be children of your Father in heaven.

MATTHEW 5:44–45

I AM DEPENDABLE AND UNCHANGING, a secure rock upon which you can anchor your heart and life. When you struggle during the storms of life, remember that the storm is temporary, but I am eternal. My Spirit offers peace to soothe you, comfort to help you overcome any difficulty you may face, and strength and hope to ease your trouble and grief. Call upon My loving presence with your song of praise and make music to Me with all your soul. My joy will overflow from your heart, and I will be your strength.

Spirit of God, empower me to love my enemies as You
love me and to pray for those who persecute me.

They were all filled with the Holy Spirit and spoke the word of God boldly.

ACTS 4:31

MY SPIRIT FILLS YOU WITH BOLDNESS—boldness to share My Word and My wisdom. He emboldens you to speak the truth in love and to share My grace and forgiveness. Eloquent speech does not impress Me; instead, I am drawn to a humble heart and willing spirit. The Holy Spirit fills you with a love for Me and others and ignites in you a desire to bring the lost to Me. When you are filled with My Spirit, your faith will be contagious as you boldly spread My gospel of love and forgiveness.

Heavenly Father, fill me to overflowing with Your Spirit so that I may speak boldly for You. Give me a love for the lost just as You loved me when I was lost.

Whoever sows to please their flesh, from the flesh will reap destruction; whoever sows to please the Spirit, from the Spirit will reap eternal life.

GALATIANS 6:8

I DESIRE FOR YOU TO GROW IN SPIRITUAL MATURITY. The law of sowing and reaping leads to life or destruction. Sowing to please the Spirit reaps eternal life, but sowing to please the flesh reaps destruction. As I sow humility into your heart, you will reap grace in your relationships. As I sow love into your soul, you will reap courage. As I sow compassion into your life, you will reap empathy. I want to protect you from the harm and destruction that comes from living apart from My Spirit. Sow a life led by the Spirit, and you will reap eternal rewards.

Heavenly Father, sow Your good seed into my life so that I may reap Your good harvest. Help me to recognize when I am living in my flesh rather than being led by Your Spirit.

Give, and it will be given to you. A good measure,
pressed down, shaken together and running over,
will be poured into your lap. For with the measure you use,
it will be measured to you.

LUKE 6:38

WHEN YOU GIVE AWAY YOUR LIFE FOR MY SAKE, you find true life in Me. You experience purpose, fulfillment, and freedom when you give yourself away. I modeled generous living by loving and forgiving you. When you love others, you more fully understand My love for you. When you forgive others, you experience My unlimited forgiveness of you. Give away your life to find the abundant life I have for you.

Heavenly Father, I want to live generously in every aspect of my life just as You so generously give to me. Empower me to love and forgive like You.

Let no debt remain outstanding, except the continuing debt to love one another, for whoever loves others has fulfilled the law.

ROMANS 13:8

I WANT TO PROTECT YOU from the chains of debt that can hinder you from freely following My life plan for you. It's not necessary to run ahead of Me; I don't want you to become ensnared in the trap of instant gratification, demanding today what you may not even want or need tomorrow. I am your provider. Wait on Me, My child, to provide for you. When you ask the Spirit to create a contentment within you, you will become flexible and unencumbered to minister where I need you most. Live only in debt to love Me and others.

Heavenly Father, teach me to be content with what I have and to trust You to provide what I need in Your timing. Protect me from the chains of bondage so that my only debt is to love You and love others.

MAY

I will ask the Father,
and he will give you another
advocate to help you and be with
you forever—the Spirit of Truth.

JOHN 14:16–17

MAY 1

*Many are the plans in a person's heart,
but it is the LORD's purpose that prevails.*

PROVERBS 19:21

MAPPING OUT YOUR FUTURE, planning your days, weeks, and months, and setting goals are a part of your natural tendency. It would seem irresponsible not to plan. You have so many dreams and plans, but so do I. I have a plan and purpose for you. Your story is part of My larger story. I weave the moments and days of your life into My tapestry, giving meaning and purpose to your life. It isn't wrong for you to plan, but be patient and don't get ahead of Me. How do you know if an idea conceived in your heart aligns with My heart? No one knows My thoughts except My Spirit—He is My source of revelation, wisdom, and power for you. Ask Him for direction, clarity, and confirmation. My purpose always involves living in relationship with Me. I am rarely early and never late, so cease striving and rest in Me as you wait. My purpose will prevail in time, and I promise it will be worth the wait.

Heavenly Father, slow me down and draw me into Your presence. Direct my heart to Your purpose for me. Give me patience to wait on You as You transform me from the inside out.

*Let the morning bring me word of your unfailing love,
for I have put my trust in you. Show me the way I should
go, for to you I entrust my life.*

PSALM 143:8

MEET ME IN THE MORNING before the noisy world
drowns out the Spirit's gentle voice. Saturate yourself in
My peace and unfailing love. Choose to trust Me as you
begin each day. I will not disappoint. I never cancel an
appointment with you—you are worth much more to
Me than your human mind can conceive. I am always on
time, always available, and always ready to patiently listen
to you. Come to Me in faith, and I will show you My way.

*Heavenly Father, keep me from tuning my ear to the
noise of the world instead of listening to Your gentle
Spirit, who will show me Your way.*

MAY 3

During the days of Jesus' life on earth, he offered up prayers and petitions with fervent cries and tears to the one who could save him from death.

HEBREWS 5:7

CRY OUT TO ME. I hear your fervent prayers and tearful petitions when you feel crushed under the weight of heavy circumstances. Beloved, I am the One who saves you and who answers your prayers. I welcome your tears and emotions during trials and times of sorrow. I am well acquainted with walking through the valley of the shadow of death; in empathy, I will walk with you. I will restore your soul and lead you to My still waters of rest. My Spirit will rejuvenate you and nourish your heart with My Word. Don't hesitate to cry out loudly, speak passionately, or whisper intimately to Me. I love you, and I alone can save you.

Heavenly Father, I trust You when I face the unknown and praise You for walking with me through the valleys of life. Thank You for leading me to still waters where I can rest in You and restore my soul.

Do not conform to the pattern of this world, but be transformed by the renewing of your mind. Then you will be able to test and approve what God's will is—his good, pleasing and perfect will.

ROMANS 12:2

MY TRANSFORMING POWER IS AT WORK IN YOU. My Spirit renews your mind and replaces the lies you believe with My truth. I exchange your old thinking with My unchanging truth in a world that is ever-changing. Rely on My Spirit, who transforms your heart and mind with My truth. The Spirit exposes the subtle conformity to the patterns of the world that can so easily creep into your belief system. Invite the Spirit to test and approve My good, pleasing, and perfect will and reveal it to you.

Holy Spirit, transform my heart and mind to recognize truth over lies. Make me new and lead me in the Father's perfect will.

*Then he opened their minds so they could
understand the Scriptures.*

LUKE 24:45

JUST AS MY SPIRIT INSPIRED the writing of Scripture,
My Spirit inspires the understanding of Scripture. Walk
closely with Me, and I will open your mind and show you
My ways. I love you as a father loves his child. The Spirit
will speak words of comfort and support to your soul as
you keep My Word close throughout the day. My Word
is alive and engaging, ready to give you what you need
when you need it.

*Heavenly Father, breathe on me the breath of Your love
and understanding. Open my heart and mind to understand the truth of Your Word.*

I will instruct you and teach you in the way you should go;
I will counsel you with my loving eye on you.

PSALM 32:8

I AM WITH YOU DURING TIMES OF TRANSITION. Trust Me more intentionally when you face uncertainty. New beginnings are a part of life and will keep your faith fresh and growing. My Word is a light for your path, and I will walk with you each step of the way. My love will sustain you as I lead you through each season of life. Though you are uncomfortable, I am still in control. My comfort will spring forth out of your discomfort. The Spirit will increase your trust in Me during the changing seasons of your life; remain confident that where I lead is best for you.

Heavenly Father, I know You are good, and I choose to trust You during times of transition. I am so very grateful that You are in control and the Spirit guides me in Your ways.

Surely God is my help;
the Lord is the one who sustains me.

PSALM 54:4

I AM YOUR SUSTAINING HELP. The Spirit gives you the spiritual stamina and physical strength to sustain your life. In crisis, the Spirit calms you. When under pressure, the Spirit gives perspective. My grace and mercy sustain you. Slow down the pace of your life to spend time with Me in prayer, and I will energize your faith in Me. Take inventory of your activities and eliminate what feels obligatory rather than purposeful in order to create margin for Me and for those whom you love most. Trust Me, beloved. I will lift you up and sustain you.

Heavenly Father, You sustain me even when I feel like I'm at the end of my rope. I humbly bow my heart before You in praise for my spiritual and physical strength.

The Kingdom of God is not a matter of what
we eat or drink, but of living a life of goodness
and peace and joy in the Holy Spirit.

ROMANS 14:17, NLT

I AM IN CONTROL of all the details of your life. Your joy is not dependent upon or determined by your circumstances, but rather by continually abiding in My presence. My kingdom will come on earth through My faithful followers who are full of peace and joy. Continually live in My presence and unconditional love. Allow My Spirit to lead, empower, and fill you so you can experience true joy.

Heavenly Father, remind me that my joy and peace are not dependent upon my circumstances. Empower me to abide in Your presence to experience Your unceasing joy and peace.

When pride comes, then comes disgrace,
but with humility comes wisdom.

PROVERBS 11:2

THE SPIRIT IS THE SOURCE OF ALL WISDOM and freely offers it to your humble heart. The world you live in applauds knowledge and success, but I applaud humility and teachability. Trying to earn the praise of people leaves you exhausted and empty. The Spirit offers peace and contentment when you trust Him to lead you. Humility is a signal that are ready for the Spirit to entrust you with My wisdom. I love you and want to reveal My wisdom to you to protect you from disgrace and pride.

Heavenly Father, I humbly seek Your wisdom so I can serve You wholeheartedly. Teach me Your ways so that I may walk in them all the days of my life.

*You were taught, with regard to your former way of life,
to put off your old self, which is being corrupted by its
deceitful desires; to be made new in the attitude of your
minds; and to put on the new self, created to be like
God in true righteousness and holiness.*

EPHESIANS 4:22–24

MY SPIRIT EMPOWERS YOU to put off your old self and
put on your new self to be like Me. As with any new habit, it takes patience and practice to become proficient at
being led by My Spirit. Just as each day you choose what
clothing to put on your physical body, each day you can
choose to align your thinking with your new mind—the
mind of Christ. The Spirit will exchange your pride with
humility, your fear with love, and your selfishness with
generosity. Dress yourself with the clothes of My character, and My beauty will be on display for all to see.

*Heavenly Father, teach me to dress in true righteous-
ness and holiness to become like You. Any beauty I possess comes from Your Spirit in me.*

Where can I go from your Spirit? Where can I flee from your presence? If I go up to the heavens, you are there; if I make my bed in the depths, you are there.
If I rise on the wings of the dawn, if I settle on the far side of the sea, even there your hand will guide me, your right hand will hold me fast.

PSALM 139:7–10

NOTHING CAN SEPARATE YOU from My presence. My Spirit lives within you—He is always with you. Sometimes you want to run and hide from Me because you feel unworthy to be in My presence because of your guilt and shame. My compassion never fails. My love is enduring. I will always pursue an intimate relationship with you. You are perfectly known and loved in every way.

Spirit of God, I take great comfort in knowing that wherever I go I will be in Your presence. Help me to run to You rather than from You when I feel unworthy.

O God, do not remain silent; do not turn a deaf ear,
do not stand aloof, O God.

PSALM 83:1

ALTHOUGH I MAY BE SILENT AT TIMES, I am always present with you. My silence may feel awkward, but My loving-kindness and compassion cover you. The Spirit dwells with you to listen and offer comfort in the same way a caring friend silently sits in your presence to console you. Rest and reflect in quietness and receive My gift of grace. Be confident of My infinite love for you even in My silence.

Heavenly Father, still my heart in the silence and reveal Your love to me. Teach me to silence the voices of doubt and despair and to receive Your grace and compassion.

Remain in me, as I also remain in you.
No branch can bear fruit by itself; it must remain in the
vine. Neither can you bear fruit unless you remain in me.

JOHN 15:4

I AM YOUR SOURCE OF LIFE. Grapes don't strive to grow; they are sustained by the vine on which they hang. So it is with you—I don't ask you to strive to perform and please Me. Quite the opposite! I simply want you to abide in Me, maintaining a constant dependence upon and communion with Me. When you dwell with Me, you draw upon My unlimited resources to accomplish what I have planned for you. When surrendered to My Spirit, you will be unencumbered and free. Don't waste your energy trying to please Me, for you can do nothing in your own strength. When you abide in Me and walk in the power of the Spirit, My burden is easy and My yoke is light.

Heavenly Father, empower me to remain in You. Gently remind me to return to You when I break away and begin living in my own strength. I give You all glory for any fruit I may bear.

When the LORD restored the fortunes of Zion, we were like those who dreamed. Our mouths were filled with laughter, our tongues with songs of joy.

PSALM 126:1–2

JOY IS FOUND IN FREEDOM IN ME. Joy is a gift the Spirit freely offers, and it isn't dependent on your circumstances. You find joy when you realize you are free from the bondage of sin. Bondage smothers your soul, but My Spirit sets you free and breathes fresh life into your soul. Celebrate your deliverance and the gift of eternal life with Me. Rejoice in the transformation of the Spirit at work in your life. Make room for the Spirit to fill your heart with My great love, joy, and laughter. I am the giver of freedom and joy. Enjoy the abundant blessing of life with Me.

Spirit of God, empower me to live free from the bondage of sin. Fill my heart with Your love, joy, and laughter.

*Have compassion on me, L*ORD*, for I am weak. Heal me,*
*L*ORD*, for my bones are in agony. I am sick at heart. How*
*long, O L*ORD*, until you restore me?*

PSALM 6:2−3, NLT

MY COMPASSION BRINGS HEALING to your troubled heart. I have not forgotten you. Because of My love, you are not consumed. My compassions never fail, and My mercies are new every morning. My Spirit restores the joy of your salvation and brings healing to your soul. I am strong in your weakness. I give rest to your tired soul. I lift you up out of the pit of loneliness and offer hope. I will show you the path of life and the fullness of My joy.

Heavenly Father, empty me of myself and fill me with Your love. Heal my heart and restore the joy of my salvation.

This is the day that the LORD has made;
let us rejoice and be glad in it.

PSALM 118:24, ESV

TODAY IS MY GIFT TO YOU. Live in the moment and trust Me for tomorrow. All you need for today can be found in Me. Don't fret and worry about what you don't have. The intentional practice of gratitude is transformational; focus on what you have—not what you think you need. My deep, abiding joy accompanies a soul satisfied in Me alone. You will experience heartfelt gladness when you allow the Spirit to guide you to accomplish My will.

Heavenly Father, I receive Your gift of today. Help me to joyfully carry out Your will in all I do today. Give me a heart of thanksgiving even in difficult times.

The righteous cry out, and the LORD hears them; he delivers them from all their troubles. The LORD is close to the brokenhearted and saves those who are crushed in spirit.

PSALM 34:17–18

HEARTACHE AND PAIN OF REJECTION ARE REAL. When people you love the most fail you, pull away and listen for the tender whisper of the Spirit reminding you that you are extravagantly loved by Me. My unconditional love and acceptance validate your utmost worth. You are My lovely creation, and I see your beauty. When you fear being unloved, turn to the Spirit for reassurance and to soothe you with truth and peace. My love for you is unwavering.

Heavenly Father, when I feel rejected and unloved, remind me of Your extravagant love for me. Heal my broken heart and help me to live out of Your mercy and grace.

If serving the L<small>ORD</small> seems undesirable to you, then choose for yourselves this day whom you will serve, whether the gods your ancestors served beyond the Euphrates, or the gods of the Amorites, in whose land you are living. But as for me and my household, we will serve the L<small>ORD</small>.

JOSHUA 24:15

YOU ARE A LIVING MODEL TO YOUR FAMILY and will leave a legacy of faith in Me when those you love see you following Me. Serving Me will cause some to sneer, others to dismiss you, and a few to admire your love for Me. Living for Me in your culture is difficult. It's why Jesus said, "Whoever wants to be my disciple must deny themselves and take up their cross and follow me." This is the very reason I gave you the gift of the Spirit to indwell and empower you. He enables you to swim against the current of the culture and follow Me.

Heavenly Father, I choose to serve You in spite of it being culturally unpopular. Empower me by Your Spirit to swim against the current and follow You.

I call on the LORD in my distress,
and he answers me.

PSALM 120:1

I LISTEN TO YOUR PRAYERS AND ANSWER when you call to Me in distress. Call to Me for comfort, and My Spirit will comfort your anxious heart. Call to Me for strength, and My Spirit will provide strength for perseverance. Call to Me for patience and forgiveness, and My Spirit will empower you to patiently love and forgive those who have hurt you. My heart goes out to you in your distress to give you rest. Call to Me.

Heavenly Father, I am grateful for Your comfort and strength when I am distressed. Your merciful love provides everything I need to withstand whatever life brings my way.

The peace of God, which transcends all understanding,
will guard your hearts and your minds in Christ Jesus.

PHILIPPIANS 4:7

I WILL GUARD YOUR HEART with My peace. Your heart is the epicenter of your emotions. The Spirit puts up guardrails of truth and grace to protect your emotions by grounding them in Me. Pride will make promises to your heart it cannot keep as it captures your emotions with selfishness, only to ruin relationships. My Spirit will lead your heart into unselfish service and fulfillment. Release your emotions to Me. Pour out your heart to Me—spare no detail—and I will lovingly care for and comfort you. I will bear your burdens, share your joy, free your heart, and provide My perfect peace.

Heavenly Father, give me the courage to open my heart completely to You. Even though my every thought is known by You, I oftentimes try to hide my true emotions from You as if I can disguise them. I trust You to guard my heart and mind in Your peace and love through Christ.

He cuts off every branch in me that bears no fruit,
while every branch that does bear fruit he prunes
so that it will be even more fruitful.

JOHN 15:2

BECAUSE I LOVE YOU, I prune and discipline you. My pruning molds and shapes you for the wonderful plans I have for your life. I don't discipline to shame or tear down; I discipline to lead you to abundant life. My discipline is intended to prepare and equip you to bear My fruit. I prune you to become more dependent on Me. I lovingly and carefully cut away unhelpful influences in your life. The Spirit gives you discernment to break off what needs to be removed. When I prune, I may remove something good, creating margin to grow something better. Trust Me to nurture you into a healthy branch that will bear much fruit for Me.

Heavenly Father, allow me to see Your discipline with an open heart and mind and to join You in the process of pruning me to produce fruit for You.

If you, L̲ᴏʀᴅ, kept a record of sins, L̲ᴏʀᴅ, who could stand?
But with you there is forgiveness, so that we can,
with reverence, serve you.

PSALM 130:3–4

MY LOVE IS FORGIVING and keeps no record of your sins. My grace pardons your past guilt, your present offenses, and your future indiscretions. My great love for you is reason not to sin against Me. When you love Me, you love what I love—holiness. The Spirit will set you apart, and the Spirit will make you holy. Since I keep no record of your wrongs, imitate My love and keep no record of others' wrongs. Love wipes the slate clean.

Heavenly Father, I am overwhelmed by Your loving forgiveness. Empower me by Your Spirit to wipe the slate clean and keep no record of others' wrongs.

Yes, my soul, find rest in God;
my hope comes from him.

PSALM 62:5

MY PRESENCE QUIETS YOUR SOUL. My love reassures you and allows you to rest in My presence. Tune your ear to My voice to drown out the voices of fear that taunt you. Abide in stillness with Me, and My Spirit will wash over you with peace and calm your emotions. Feel My embrace and rest in My compassion. I'm right here with you. I am in control. Place your trust in Me, for I am your salvation and hope.

Heavenly Father, teach me to hear Your voice above all others. I receive Your comfort and care as I enter into Your presence and embrace Your steadfast love.

*In Christ Jesus you are all children of God
through faith, for all of you who were baptized into
Christ have clothed yourselves with Christ.*

GALATIANS 3:26–27

YOUR SIGNIFICANCE COMES FROM ME. I adopted you as My child because of your faith in My Son, Jesus. The Spirit continues to transform you into My image, reflecting your new identity as My child. My strength becomes your strength. My love becomes your love. My patience becomes your patience. My joy becomes your joy. You become My representative, and the Spirit empowers you to love others as I love you. When you love others with My love, you will reflect an inner beauty that draws others to you and points them to Me.

Heavenly Father, create in me a clean heart and clothe me with Your love and grace. Fill me with Your Spirit so that I can put Your love on display.

*The LORD gives wisdom; from his mouth
come knowledge and understanding.*

PROVERBS 2:6

I LONG FOR YOU TO UNDERSTAND ME AND MY WAYS.
My indwelling Spirit breathes discernment into you and
guides you to Me. He won't leave you in the dark—He
lights your path with and leads you into wisdom. My
Word provides wisdom, and My Spirit leads you into
understanding. I do not hide from you—I make Myself
known to you. Knowing Me intimately leads to understanding who I am.

*Heavenly Father, light my path and impart Your wis-
dom and understanding to me. I want to intimately
know You and implicitly trust You.*

Be on your guard; stand firm in the faith;
be courageous; be strong.

1 CORINTHIANS 16:13

MY SPIRIT EMPOWERS YOU with courage and strength to stand firm in your faith. He guides you into truth and understanding. He empowers you to courageously stand for what's right and stand against what's wrong. Your faith will face opposition from the culture around you, but the Spirit will strengthen you and give you courage to remain steadfast. My wisdom guards your mind, and My peace guards your heart.

Holy Spirit, give me courage to stand firm when faced with temptation or opposition. Guide me into under-standing by opening my heart and mind to truth.

I pour out before him my complaint;
before him I tell my trouble.

PSALM 142:2

I AM A SAFE PLACE FOR YOU. You can safely pour out your complaints to Me. Bring Me your burdens and troubles so I can carry them for you. Cry out to Me from the depths of your heart. My Spirit leads you into My presence and comforts you in your distress. Bring all of yourself to Me. I give you permission to vent your frustrations to Me, lay your raw questions before Me, and come to Me unhindered so your soul does not stew in bitterness. I am not afraid of your questions and doubts. The Spirit guides you in truth, leads you to understanding, and offers peace for your soul.

Heavenly Father, thank You for giving me permission to cry out to You in times of trouble and to bring my doubts and questions before You. Lead me to Your truth that will set me free.

*Everyone who hears these words of mine
and puts them into practice is like a wise man who built
his house on the rock. But everyone who hears
these words of mine and does not put them into practice
is like a foolish man who built his house on sand.*

MATTHEW 7:24, 26

I AM YOUR SOLID ROCK, your refuge and strength. My Word is the blueprint for your life. When you put My Word into practice, you build your life on a solid foundation. Taking shortcuts may bring short-term satisfaction, but when the storms of life begin to blow, your character will crumble. Developing godly character takes time. A life built on the foundation of My Word and guidance from the Spirit will withstand any storm. As you walk in My ways, you will forge a life of hope and joy far better than an empty, superficial, and fleeting life.

Heavenly Father, I desire to live a life built on the foundation of Your Word. Teach me Your ways and empower me to live fully surrendered to You.

I remember the days of long ago; I meditate on all your works and consider what your hands have done.

PSALM 143:5

MEDITATING ON MY PAST FAITHFULNESS will bring you peace. My deeds of long ago are worth remembering and will increase your faith in Me and My possibilities. Celebrate My work of salvation—how you were once blind, but now you see. Meditate on My faithfulness and the prayers I have answered. Delight in the lives of those you love who have come to a saving knowledge of Me. Rejoice over the health I've restored, the relationships I've healed, and how I have provided for you and your family. Ask the Spirit to help you recall My faithfulness and the many ways I have provided for you, protected you, and answered your prayers. As you consider My past faithfulness, you will be filled with hope and peace for your future.

Heavenly Father, I celebrate You and Your work in my life. Consistently bring to my mind the many ways You have faithfully provided for me and answered my prayers. Let Your hope spill over onto those around me.

Jesus replied, "You do not realize now what I am doing,
but later you will understand."

JOHN 13:7

YOU MAY NOT SEE ME AT WORK IN YOUR LIFE NOW,
but later you will understand. Sometimes My love prevents Me from revealing too much and overwhelming
you. Rest in My goodness and trust in My faithfulness.
When you feel uncertainty creep into your heart, communicate your fears to Me, and ask the Spirit to cast out
your fear with My perfect love. Meditate on My truth and
remember My faithfulness in your life. I am always in control. I know your past, I am with you in the present, and I
see your future. Trust Me and know that when you look
back, you will see that you were not alone.

Heavenly Father, help me to grow my faith and be con-
fident in You even when I don't understand what You
are doing. Teach me to meditate on Your perfect love
that casts out all fear and to rely on Your Spirit to lead
me out of darkness and into Your light.

Trust in the LORD with all your heart
And do not lean on your own understanding.
In all your ways acknowledge Him,
And He will make your paths straight.

PROVERBS 3:5–6, NASB

I PROVIDE A GOOD WAY FOR YOU. When you come to a crossroads, ask My Spirit for wisdom. He will walk with you as you discover My ways. My Word will instruct you, and the life of My Son is a model for you. Jesus chose to serve over being served. He gave power away instead of abusing it. He lived simply rather than affluently. As you create mental margin to meditate on My truth, your thoughts will reflect My thoughts. My Spirit will guide you into wisdom and understanding and lead you in My ways.

Heavenly Father, give me faith to trust You and wisdom to follow You.

JUNE

I pray that out of his glorious riches he may strengthen you with power through his Spirit in your inner being, so that Christ may dwell in your hearts through faith.

EPHESIANS 3:16–17

Whatever you do, do it all for the glory of God.

1 CORINTHIANS 10:31

I AM WITH YOU IN EVERYTHING YOU DO. My Spirit enables you to live a life that brings glory to Me. I receive glory when your life reflects Me to others. I receive glory when you make wise choices after seeking My will. I receive glory when you forgive a person who intentionally hurts you. I receive glory when you display humility and generously serve others with your time and resources. I am with you in all you do, and I find pleasure when you serve Me.

Heavenly Father, I pray that others will see my life and recognize that You are with me in everything I do. I give You all the glory for what You accomplish through me.

JUNE 2

The LORD upholds all those who fall and lifts up all who are bowed down.

PSALM 145:14

I UPHOLD YOU WHEN YOU FALL and use your brokenness for your good. I am the God of second chances. My grace gives you room for failure so you can learn and grow. My love allows you to turn from fear and move forward by faith in Me. My mercy and peace assure you that I'm with you. My Spirit gives you strength to persevere when you feel you can't go further and lifts you up when you bow down in humble praise to Me.

Heavenly Father, I bow down to You in my weakness and ask You to lift me up in Your strength. Enable me to persevere in Your power and give You all the glory.

*I will ask the Father, and he will give you another
advocate to help you and be with you forever—the Spirit
of truth. The world cannot accept him, because it
neither sees him nor knows him. But you know him,
for he lives with you and will be in you.*

JOHN 14:16–17

LIFE IS FULL OF CHALLENGES greater than you can handle on your own. Because I knew you would face things beyond your capability, I sent you a helper and an advocate. He supports you in difficult situations. When you face confusion, He sorts things out and gives you clarity, insight, and truth. When you want to give up, He provides strength and courage. When you are overwhelmed by decisions, He counsels you with wisdom. When you face temptations that are impossible to resist on your own, He empowers you to faithfully follow Me. He is your constant companion, interceding on your behalf. He is your Comforter, offering peace in the midst of any challenge you face.

Heavenly Father, thank You for the Spirit—my Counselor, Comforter, Helper, and Advocate. Teach me to recognize His voice and help me follow wherever He leads.

*Command those who are rich in this present
world not to be arrogant nor to put their
hope in wealth, which is so uncertain, but to put
their hope in God, who richly provides.*

1 TIMOTHY 6:17

PUT YOUR HOPE IN ME rather than the fleeting riches this world offers. I richly provide for you with My dependable reliability. Money may be here today and gone tomorrow, but you can count on My faithfulness regardless of your circumstances. Hoping in riches leads to unfulfillment, but hoping in Me is a confident expectation of the assurance I offer. Hope comes from the power of the Holy Spirit allowing you to trust Me, which leads to joy and peace.

Heavenly Father, my hope is in You, and all I have belongs to You. Thank You for being faithful and trustworthy and richly providing for me.

One thing I ask of the Lord, this only do I seek: that I may dwell in the house of the Lord all the days of my life, to gaze upon the beauty of the Lord and to seek him in his temple.

PSALM 27:4

YOU BRING ME GREAT PLEASURE when you desire to be with Me in stillness and worship. When you seek Me with a sincere heart, I am easily found. My Spirit will lead you to Me all the days of your life. I created a world of beauty for you see and experience. You will see My handiwork as you gaze upon the beauty of nature. The magnificence of a tiny baby or an aging adult growing in grace is My beauty on display. Behold My beauty when My followers gather to worship Me and attest to My love and holiness. Come and dwell with Me forever.

Heavenly Father, there is no better place to be than in Your presence. Thank You for creating beauty to point me to You.

In vain you rise early and stay up late,
toiling for food to eat—for he grants sleep to those he loves.

PSALM 127:2

SLEEP IS A GIFT TO THOSE I LOVE. I delight when you sleep soundly in My peace. I speak over you in the night, and the Spirit communes with your spirit as you rest. My calming presence allows your soul to recover and be strengthened. Striving and toiling will not produce success, but sleeping while trusting Me restores you physically, emotionally, and spiritually. You can wholly depend on Me to provide for your every need.

Heavenly Father, thank You for the gift of sleep. Remind me when I am tempted to overwork—cramming too much into my day—that I can rest in You because I trust You to take care of my needs.

JUNE 7

My dear brothers and sisters, take note of this:
Everyone should be quick to listen,
slow to speak and slow to become angry.

JAMES 1:19

MY WISDOM WILL HAVE YOU REMAIN QUIET at times, especially in the face of unfair criticism. It is so much easier to share your opinion or your side of the story than to actively listen to others. It is difficult to not respond emotionally and try to defend yourself. The only way you can patiently wait on Me in silence is by yielding to My Spirit. I always bring to light the truth in My timing. I fight spiritual battles unseen by human eyes—only those with eyes of faith can see Me at work. My work in your life will become more evident over time. I love you, and I see you. I am your shield and defender.

Spirit of God, empower me not to respond emotionally when I am hurt or angry. Help me to demonstrate Your love by learning to be quick to listen and slow to speak.

Even though Jesus was God's Son, he learned obedience
from the things he suffered. In this way, God qualified
him as a perfect High Priest, and he became the source
of eternal salvation for all those who obey him.

HEBREWS 5:8-9, NLT

SUFFERING IS A CLASSROOM TO TEACH OBEDIENCE.
What the Spirit teaches you during suffering is remembered more vividly than what you learn in less demanding times. When you view suffering in light of eternity, the Spirit reminds you that I work all things for the good of those who love Me. I will use your trials to accomplish My will. The Spirit will draw you to Me and strengthen you when you feel you can't go further. I desire for you to know Me, love Me, and obey Me, even in the midst of your suffering. The Spirit will comfort you and help you persevere as He gently leads you through the storm.

Heavenly Father, I struggle to see You when I'm suffering. Please open my spiritual eyes so I can see You in the midst of my trials. Give me the strength and courage to remain steadfast and faithful to You no matter what may come.

*Pray for us. We are sure that we have a clear conscience
and desire to live honorably in every way.*

HEBREWS 13:18

A CLEAR CONSCIENCE PAVES THE PATH to intimacy
with Me. Unconfessed sin eats away at you, grieves the
Spirit, and hinders your prayers. Your physical, emotional,
and relational well-being will suffer when you refuse to
confess to Me. Confession is My invitation for you to lay
your shame and guilt at the foot of the cross and walk
away with a clean heart. It reunites My heart to yours.
When you are willing to expose to Me all that is in your
heart, it removes the barriers in our relationship. You
have nothing to hide from Me—I love you so much that
I paid the price for your sin so we can have an intimate
relationship. My grace frees your conscience from past
guilt and frees you to give grace and forgiveness to others. When your conscience is clear, the Spirit ushers in My
supernatural peace.

*Heavenly Father, help me to keep short accounts and a
clear conscience. I praise You for the gift of forgiveness
and the freedom and peace You offer when I confess
and repent.*

My soul thirsts for God, for the living God.
When can I go and meet with God?

PSALM 42:2

I AM YOUR SOURCE OF PLEASURE and contentment. You always have an open invitation to meet with Me. You can meet Me in the quiet of the morning or during the chaos of your hectic day. There are no rigid rules or formulas for how and when to spend time with Me. I am with you wherever you go. Come to Me when you are ashamed or hurt, lonely or depressed, fearful or burdened. My Spirit will nurture your soul, and I will heal your broken and discouraged heart. I alone can satisfy your need for unconditional love and acceptance. I am a never-ending source of living water to refresh and restore your love-thirsty soul. Slow down, drink from Me, and stay awhile.

Heavenly Father, quench my thirsty soul with Your satisfying love. Remind me to slow down and drink from Your living water throughout my day. Refresh and restore my heart so Your love may spill over onto those around me.

Repent at my rebuke! Then I will pour out my thoughts to you, I will make known to you my teachings.

PROVERBS 1:23

I WANT TO POUR OUT MY HEART AND THOUGHTS and lead you into wisdom. You will experience the benefits of a relationship with Me when you listen to the Spirit and accept My correction. I discipline those I love to prevent them from floundering in foolish behavior. My redemptive reproach is a reflection of My holiness, which cannot coexist with sin. I don't condemn you. No—I call you out of sin and back to intimacy with Me. My forgiveness makes you white as snow, and My Spirit will pour out My love and wisdom on you.

Heavenly Father, thank You for gently convicting me in love and calling me back to You. I want no barrier in my relationship with You. I desire Your love and wisdom.

Rejoice always, pray continually, give thanks in all circumstances; for this is God's will for you in Christ Jesus.

1 THESSALONIANS 5:16–18

GIVING THANKS IN ALL CIRCUMSTANCES is My will for you. This is impossible in your own strength, but the Spirit enables you to continually live with a heart of gratitude. I'm not asking you to give thanks *for* your circumstances; I'm asking you to give thanks *in* all circumstances. When you praise Me with a grateful heart, whatever consumes you diminishes, and the Spirit is free to reveal Me to you. When you face pain and problems and disappointments, relying on the Spirit to empower you to give thanks takes your eyes off of yourself and directs your heart and attention to Me. Once I have your attention, the Spirit produces joy and peace in you in spite of your circumstances. Gratitude is My gift to you and helps you draw near to Me.

Heavenly Father, I want to give thanks in all things. Help me to live with an attitude of gratitude no matter the circumstance and experience Your joy and peace.

If the Son sets you free, you will be free indeed.

JOHN 8:36

YOU ARE FREE. My Son paid for your freedom on the cross, and My Spirit breaks your chains of bondage. You are free from the power of sin. You are free from guilt and shame. You are free to love unconditionally and forgive completely. You are free to trust and follow Me. You are free to abide in Me and walk in the power of the Spirit. My freedom is a gift—not to be taken for granted but to be guarded and used for My glory. The Spirit leads you to freedom in Me. Enjoy your freedom!

Heavenly Father, fill me with the power of the Spirit to help me regard Your freedom as freedom to live the life to which You've called me.

*I am the vine; you are the branches. If you remain
in me and I in you, you will bear much fruit;
apart from me you can do nothing.*

JOHN 15:5

YOU WILL BEAR MUCH FRUIT IF YOU REMAIN IN ME.
Utter dependence on Me will yield lasting fruit in your
life. Remain in Me by constantly communing with the
Spirit in prayer. I don't intend for you to go through
your day mustering the energy and strength to serve Me.
When you stay connected to Me, the Spirit will give you
all the sustenance and strength you need to do what I
call you to do. Give the Spirit the freedom to direct your
steps and lead you where I would have you go. I am always with you—stay close to Me.

*Heavenly Father, direct not only my steps, but also my
mind and heart. I want to remain connected to You so
Your life can flow through me.*

*Praise be to the God and Father of our
Lord Jesus Christ, the Father of compassion
and the God of all comfort, who comforts us in all our
troubles, so that we can comfort those in any trouble
with the comfort we ourselves receive from God.*

2 CORINTHIANS 1:3–4

I COMFORT YOU in all your troubles. There is no trouble you face that My comfort and compassion can't transform and use for My glory. My Spirit desires to replace your fear with peace. My compassion is able to convert your pain into passion to serve Me. My comfort enters your mess and lifts you up out of the miry clay onto the solid rock of My love. Remember the comfort and compassion I shower on you so when you encounter someone experiencing trouble, you can be a vessel of My comfort and compassion to them.

Heavenly Father, I praise You for Your comfort and compassion. Help me to soak it in so that I may pass it on to other broken hearts.

The word of the Lord endures forever.

1 PETER 1:25

MY ENDURING WORD is your playbook for life. It is like a love letter from Me—the story of My unceasing pursuit of you. My Word introduces you to who I am and describes My intense love for you. Ask the Spirit to open the eyes of your heart so you may know Me better through My Word. My Word is living and active and like no other book. It is the source of truth that transforms your heart and mind. My Word brings comfort in times of pain, wisdom in times of confusion, and hope to a hurting world. Meet Me in My Word—My Spirit will speak to you through it, and you will discover that it is the best-spent time of your day.

Heavenly Father, Your Word is a precious gift. Thank You for preserving it through the ages so that I may know You. Give me an unquenchable thirst to spend time with You in Your Word.

But he said to me, "My grace is sufficient for you,
for my power is made perfect in weakness."
Therefore I will boast all the more gladly about my
weaknesses, so that Christ's power may rest on me.

2 CORINTHIANS 12:9

YOUR WEAKNESS IS AN OPPORTUNITY for Me to make you strong. Your vulnerability invites Me to set you free from pride and pretense, so name your struggles out loud. My Spirit will help you define your weaknesses to make you better aware of your blind spots. Refrain from being defensive about your flaws—they provide a stage upon which My power can be displayed. When you embrace your imperfections, you open yourself to the empowerment of the Spirit to work in and through you. I am exalted in your life when I transform your weaknesses into My strength.

Heavenly Father, help me to acknowledge my weaknesses so You can perfect Your power in me.

JUNE 18

The Lord gives strength to his people;
the Lord blesses his people with peace.

PSALM 29:11

I SHOWER YOU WITH BOUNTIFUL BLESSINGS. Strength and peace are gifts from Me. Fear is an obstacle to what I desire for you. When you surrender to Me, the Holy Spirit covers you with peace and leads you in My ways. When you feel you are at the end of yourself, the Spirit gives strength to persevere. When you are overcome with anxiety, when relationships are strained, when your life appears to be falling apart, My Spirit ushers in My inner tranquility and resolve to calm your tired and shattered heart. I am well aware, precious child, of the weariness of the world, but I have overcome the world.

Heavenly Father, steer my heart to You when I am weak and distressed. I celebrate Your blessings of peace and strength—they truly are sweet gifts from You.

My dear brothers and sisters, be strong and immovable. Always work enthusiastically for the Lord, for you know that nothing you do for the Lord is ever useless.

1 CORINTHIANS 15:58, NLT

WHAT YOU DO IN MY NAME IS NEVER WASTED. You are My masterpiece, and the Spirit will produce good work through you. But what you do does not define you. I value you, not because of what you do for Me, but because you are Mine. Let nothing and no one move you away from Me. When you fully give yourself to Me and My plans for you, you can be confident that your work for Me is not futile. Your work is a platform to showcase Me at work in you. As I serve you, you serve others. What you do for Me is never in vain, it is a sweet offering.

Heavenly Father, thank You for loving me, not because of what I do, but because I am Yours. Help me to remain steadfast in serving You and to always give myself fully to Your work.

JUNE 20

In all these things we are more than conquerors
through him who loved us.

ROMANS 8:37

I KNOW YOU BY NAME. I know the struggles you face every day. My Spirit empowers you to be an overcomer. You may experience overwhelming, intense conflict, but be confident that I know what you need. When you need assurance, I am your security. When you need acceptance, I am your friend. When you need approval, I am your encourager. My Spirit works in you and helps you overcome all obstacles. Your struggles allow Me to expand your capacity to love and grow your heart of humility.

Heavenly Father, help me not to lose sight of Your deep love for me in the midst of my struggles. I invite Your Spirit to work in and through me to overcome the struggles and obstacles I face.

JUNE 21

Be alert and of sober mind. Your enemy the devil prowls around like a roaring lion looking for someone to devour.

1 PETER 5:8

I LONG FOR YOUR FAITH TO FLOURISH. Open your heart and mind to My Spirit, and He will increase your faith. The Enemy is the accuser and seeks to devour you. I am your Father, and My Spirit of Truth lives in you. Don't try to fight spiritual battles without My Spirit. He gives you a way of escape when you are tempted and empowers you to overcome any temptation. Rely on the Spirit to combat the Enemy and his attempts to lure you away from Me with schemes, shortcuts, or sin. I am your security—your defender and deliverer. You can take refuge in Me. Rest in the safety of being My child.

Heavenly Father, I praise You for growing my faith in You. Equip me to recognize the traps of the Enemy so I can stand firm in You.

*Jesus answered her, "If you knew the gift of God
and who it is that asks you for a drink, you would have
asked him and he would have given you living water."*

JOHN 4:10

I AM LIVING WATER and will quench your thirsty soul.
When your heart becomes dehydrated, slow down and
experience My love and forgiveness to revive and restore
your parched soul. You will not find satisfaction in what
the world offers, but the Spirit will pour out My living water like streams in the desert and bring hope to your heart.
Receive My gift of living water that wells up to eternal life.

*Heavenly Father, lead me to Your deep well of love.
Teach me to know the difference between the empty
pleasures the world offers and the true contentment I
can find only in You.*

"Come," [Jesus] replied, "and you will see."
So they went and saw where he was staying,
and they spent that day with him.

JOHN 1:39

TIME SPENT WITH ME will help you follow Me more closely. When you spend time with Me, you discover more of who I am and grow to be more like Me. My Spirit trains you to recognize the many ways I love you and opens your spiritual ears to hear My still, quiet voice. He gives you eyes to see Me and a discerning heart to understand My ways. Accept My invitation to be with Me—it is not burdensome and taxing, but life-giving and healing. The Spirit teaches you how to love like I do. He offers My grace to the rich and the poor—to the lost and broken—so you can lead them to the true riches that are found only in Me.

Heavenly Father, I humbly offer myself to You. Create in me an insatiable hunger to spend time with You every day so I may become more like You.

I keep my eyes always on the LORD.
With him at my right hand, I will not be shaken.

PSALM 16:8

NOTHING CAN SHAKE YOU WHEN YOU CLING TO ME. I hold the universe in My hands, telling the sun when to rise and set. In the same way, I hold your life together in My hands—even in your brokenness and chaos. People and circumstances out of your control will not undermine your faith in Me when you focus your eyes on My unfailing love. Release your imagined sense of control, allowing My Spirit to order your steps and show you what's next. Hold tight to My hand, trust My love, and always look up.

Heavenly Father, I give You the reins of my life. Turn my eyes back to You when I begin to sink because I am looking around instead of looking up to You.

For you know the grace of our Lord Jesus Christ, that
though he was rich, yet for your sake he became poor, so that
you through his poverty might become rich.

2 CORINTHIANS 8:9

THE RICHES OF MY GRACE MAKE YOU RICH IN GRACE. I descended from the heavens and became poor for your sake. I rescued and redeemed you, and I call you My own. I laid down My Son's life for you so that you would come alive for Me. I gave you the free gift of eternal life so that you may share it with those who don't know Me. I am your inspiration to give yourself away and to lead the lost to Me so that they may know that I am the Way, the Truth, and the Life. By the power of the Spirit living in you, leverage the riches of grace I've given you so others can know Me and be known by Me.

Heavenly Father, thank You for rescuing and redeem-
ing me and giving me Your riches of grace. Give me the
courage and power to lavish Your riches on those who
don't know You.

*God has spoken plainly, and I have heard
it many times: Power, O God, belongs to you;
unfailing love, O Lord, is yours.*

PSALM 62:11–12, NLT

MY POWER IS FOR YOUR BENEFIT. When you cease striving for power, you are able to rest in My control. Power feeds pride, and pride feeds power. My unfailing love coupled with My power is the perfect balance of protection and care for you. Trust My Spirit to steer your life in the best direction. Relinquish control and cease grasping for unharnessed power that will lead you away from Me. My unfailing love will draw you back to Me and is steadfast, healing, and a source of refuge.

Heavenly Father, Your power and protection provide peace for my soul, and Your unfailing love tethers me to Your heart. I willingly give You control to work in me, through me, and on my behalf.

*I know what it is to be in need, and I know what it is to
have plenty. I have learned the secret of being content
in any and every situation, whether well fed or hungry,
whether living in plenty or in want.*

PHILIPPIANS 4:12

CONTENTMENT COMES FROM TRUSTING ME to meet
your every need. The Spirit wants to teach you the secret of being content. Recognizing and relying on Me as
your provider will lead you to contentment. Completely
depend on Me to meet your needs. I am faithful and will
provide for you in creative ways that will surprise you.
Don't strive for what you don't have; rather, enjoy what I
give you, knowing it is what you need. Above all, be satisfied in My immeasurable love.

*Heavenly Father, thank You for so generously provid-
ing for me. Help me to learn the secret of being content
in what You give me and satisfied with Your love.*

And now, Lord God, keep forever the promise you have made concerning your servant and his house. Do as you promised, so that your name will be great forever.

2 SAMUEL 7:25–26

I AM FAITHFUL to keep My promises to you. I don't promise an easy life, but I give you My Spirit to shepherd you through this life. Life is full of uncertainty, but you can be certain of Me. I promise that your salvation is secure in My love and forgiveness. With every temptation, I promise to provide a way out. I promise I will never leave you or forsake you. I promise to return for you. I promise that My Word is true and trustworthy. I promise to generously give you wisdom when you ask. I promise to finish the good work I began in you. I am faithful and trustworthy and always keep My promises to My people. Anchor your life in Me. I promise you won't regret it.

Heavenly Father, Your promises provide such hope and peace. I praise You for being my promise maker and promise keeper.

"For my thoughts are not your thoughts,
neither are your ways my ways," declares the LORD.
"As the heavens are higher than the earth,
so are my ways higher than your ways
and my thoughts than your thoughts."

ISAIAH 55:8–9

WHEN I ASK YOU to do something that appears unreasonable, trust that My ways are always best for you. Human logic doesn't always align with My divine plan. Risk being misunderstood on My behalf. Tune in to the voice of the Spirit and tune out those who offer opinions and answers that don't line up with My Word. I may ask something unusual of you to ensure that I receive the glory when it is accomplished. You can trust My unconventional ways, and your faith pleases Me.

Heavenly Father, help me to trust You even when I don't understand. Give me ears to hear You and courage to follow wherever You lead.

Be strong and take heart,
all you who hope in the LORD.

PSALM 31:24

THERE IS HOPE IN YOUR FUTURE when you place your hope in Me. There are many things in which you can place your hope—wealth, family, career, power—but none will give you a deep and abiding hope. Ignore thoughts of hopelessness and allow My Spirit to lead you to the hope of love, peace, and forgiveness. You can anticipate a hopeful future in My love. I am your living hope!

Heavenly Father, nothing compares to You. I put my hope and faith in You, my Savior and Lord.

JULY

*I tell you the truth: it is to your
advantage that I go away,
for if I do not go away,
the Helper will not come to you.
But if I go, I will send him to you.*

JOHN 16:7, ESV

When he, the Spirit of truth, comes,
he will guide you into all the truth.
He will not speak on his own; he will speak only what he
hears, and he will tell you what is yet to come.

JOHN 16:13

TRANSFORMATION, NOT INFORMATION, is what I want for you. You live in the information age, and the world is exploding with knowledge. But people don't need more knowledge to transform them. They need the truth, which will set them free in Me. The Spirit gives insight and understanding. He is My secure source of wisdom, speaking only what He hears from Me. He is your guide, leading the way, and makes things clear.

Heavenly Father, help me to recognize worldly wisdom
so that I won't be led astray. Guide me into Your truth
by the power of Your Spirit.

*The LORD is close to the brokenhearted and saves
those who are crushed in spirit.*

PSALM 34:18

EMOTIONAL PAIN CAN CRUSH YOUR SPIRIT. I draw close to you when you suffer. The deep pain of betrayal can cause you to question everything and distrust everyone. I am close to you when you are at your lowest. Don't allow human failings to deceive you about Me. When a loved one ceases to love you, cling to My unceasing love. I am faithful and trustworthy. My Word is reliable and true. The Spirit consoles you and offers comfort and healing. Allow Him to lead you into deeper intimacy with Me when you are crushed in spirit. Turn to Me rather than bitterness and anger. My unlimited supply of grace and mercy is available to you. Come and rest in My arms.

Heavenly Father, my heavy heart needs Your soothing love and mercy. You alone offer unconditional love and lasting peace. I draw my strength from Your faithfulness and trustworthiness.

The joy of the LORD is your strength.

NEHEMIAH 8:10

MY JOY IS YOUR STRENGTH. I am fully aware of your imperfections and sin, yet I still choose you. I delight in you, even as My Spirit continues to perfect your faith. My joy fuels your faith and generates genuine gladness. I am forgiving, gracious, and compassionate. When you delight in My joy, it releases you from guilt and shame. My joy infuses you with comfort, strength, and peace. It is a fruit of the Spirit and cannot be displaced based on circumstances. You can experience joy in the midst of sorrow. Take hold of My joy!

Spirit of God, help me not to confuse happiness with joy. Infuse me with the joy of the Lord as You strengthen me and perfect my faith.

JULY 4

*It is God who arms me with strength
and keeps my way secure.*

PSALM 18:32

MY SPIRIT STRENGTHENS YOU for life's journey. Fatigue and discouragement can assault you like a bandit on a deserted dirt road. Life constantly swings punches at you, but My love is a healing balm. Slow down. Sit with Me. Allow My Spirit to renew your faith through rest and exchange your exhaustion for My energy. Faith in Me increases your stamina. The Spirit heals your heart, strengthens your mind, and encourages your soul. You are strong and secure in Me.

Heavenly Father, give me strength to continue my journey and faith to walk out Your calling on my life. I can handle anything life throws at me because I am secure in You.

JULY 5

He has shown you, O mortal, what is good.
*And what does the L*ORD *require of you? To act justly and to*
love mercy and to walk humbly with your God.

MICAH 6:8

JUSTICE, MERCY, AND HUMILITY are woven into the fabric of who I am. As you grow in My grace and character, your heart will change and become more like Mine. Act justly by fighting injustice and living in light of My ways rather than the world's. Stand up for what's right and speak out against what's wrong. Protect the innocent and care for the poor. Show love and mercy to all. Remain loyal to Me by loving Me with all your heart, mind, and soul. Walk in humility with a heart like Mine. Live in dependence on Me, recognizing that what you do for Me in your own strength has no eternal value—only what you accomplish by the power of the Spirit has eternal impact. Don't waste your time and energy trying to please Me. Instead, let the Spirit empower you to accomplish My will.

Heavenly Father, grow in me a heart like Yours—one that is just, mercifully loving, and humble. Give me courage to live in a way that goes against culture and radically loves others.

196

Those who know Your name will put their trust in You,
For You, LORD, have not abandoned those who seek You.

PSALM 9:10, NASB

I HAVE MANY NAMES. The Great I AM. The Most High God. The Lord Our Righteousness. Almighty God. Prince of Peace. God with Us. The Good Shepherd. Healer. Everlasting God. Provider. Bread of Life. My names tell of who I am. Those who know My name trust Me, understanding that I am full of grace, unrivaled in power, exceedingly generous, kind and compassionate, holy and just, and boundless in love. Invite the Spirit to reveal My loving-kindness and goodness to you. I AM who I AM, Your holy Redeemer and your loving Savior.

Heavenly Father, Your name is high and lifted up—the Name above all names. I wholly put my trust in You. Thank You for revealing Yourself to me and saving me by Your grace.

*Peter replied, "Repent and be baptized, every one of you,
in the name of Jesus Christ for the forgiveness of your sins.
And you will receive the gift of the Holy Spirit."*

ACTS 2:38

YOU RECEIVED THE PERMANENT GIFT of My Holy Spirit
when you first believed in Me. The Spirit offers assurance
of salvation and affirms your identity as My child. He is
your Helper, Comforter, Guide, and Counselor. He comes
alongside you to lead, encourage, and exhort. My Spirit is
the revealer of truth, guiding you into truth and enabling
you to understand My Word. He empowers you to boldly proclaim the truth of My gospel to a lost and hurting
world. I don't ask you to live a Christlike life in your own
power; I ask you to allow the Spirit to produce the life of
Christ in you. He will dwell with you forever—never leaving or forsaking you. My Spirit is a gift to you—the best
gift you will ever receive.

*Heavenly Father, the Holy Spirit is the best gift I have
ever received! Teach me not to quench Your work in my
life, but to give You more control of my life.*

Walk with the wise and become wise,
for a companion of fools suffers harm.

PROVERBS 13:20

WISDOM IS BETTER THAN RICHES AND WEALTH. Choose your friends carefully, for the company you keep can profit you or harm you. Foolish friends will lead you to destruction, but wise friends will point you to Me and help you grow in wisdom. The best source of wisdom is the Spirit. Walk with Him and ask Him to reveal My wisdom, as all wisdom flows from Me. I want to make you wise and keep you from all harm. Stay close to the Spirit, and He will stay close to you.

Heavenly Father, show me Your ways so that I may walk with You. Give me Your wisdom so that I may know You better.

Let everything that has breath praise the LORD.
Praise the LORD.

PSALM 150:6

FIX YOUR EYES ON ME and give Me praise. The Spirit urges you to praise Me because there is power in your praise and acknowledgement that I am worthy. Praise Me to dismantle worry and anxiety over your circumstances and to intentionally focus on Me. Declaring My sovereignty replaces fear with peace. Praise invites My presence into your heart and dispels any darkness that looms over you. My Spirit ushers in hope and joy. He restores and strengthens you. Praise won't fix your problems, but it changes you. The Spirit is calling you. Come and praise.

Heavenly Father, I praise You with my heart. I praise You with my head. I praise You with my breath. You alone are worthy of my praise.

JULY 10

About the gifts of the Spirit, brothers and sisters,
I do not want you to be uninformed.

1 CORINTHIANS 12:1

MY SPIRIT IS A GIFT GIVER. His gifts are for My glory. He distributes spiritual gifts to empower you to enlighten, encourage, and comfort My children. I want you to experience joy-producing pleasure when you serve Me. You will find meaning and purpose when you experience the thrill and joy of the Spirit enabling you to use your gifts to bring Me glory. I uniquely created you, and you have a special role in My story—no one else can play your part. I delight in seeing My glory on display in your life when the Spirit is at work in you. Faithfully follow Me and enter into My joy.

Spirit of God, thank You for entrusting me with spiritual gifts I can use for Your purposes. Empower me to courageously exercise my gifts.

Seek the LORD and his strength;
seek his presence continually!

PSALM 105:4, ESV

MY PRESENCE IS YOUR STRENGTH. Your eagerness to know My ways brings Me great joy. The Spirit reveals Me to you and strengthens your faith as you continue to diligently pursue Me. Humbly seek My presence and My strength. Acknowledge your dependence on Me and ask for help. Don't be afraid to share your heart with Me. I am the answer to your every problem and your every need. I long to spend time with you. Simply enjoy being in My presence. When you seek Me, you will find Me. I'll be right here waiting.

Heavenly Father, I want to seek You with all my heart. Plant in me an unrelenting desire to spend intimate time with You because I know I will never be the same after being in Your presence.

*The Lord God called to the man, and said to him,
"Where are you?" He said, "I heard the sound of You
in the garden, and I was afraid."*

GENESIS 3:9–10, NASB

DON'T BE AFRAID to come to Me just as you are. Nothing is hidden from Me, so you don't need to play hide and seek. You can relax, knowing that I am waiting with open arms for your return to Me. I paid the ultimate price to take away your shame and guilt—don't allow sin to create a barrier in our relationship. My forgiveness is a gift waiting to be received. The Enemy tries to deceive you into believing you are unworthy of My love, but the Spirit empowers you to reject his lies. I have removed your sins as far as the east is from the west. Allow My Spirit to engulf you with peace. I love you, My child. Meet Me in the quiet, and I will restore your soul.

Good Father, I am undeserving of Your love and forgiveness—but that's what makes it extravagant. Thank You for washing me whiter than snow and embracing me with arms open wide.

My sheep listen to my voice;
I know them, and they follow me.

JOHN 10:27

I SPEAK TO HUMBLE AND WILLING HEARTS when they are ready to listen. With time and practice, you'll be able to more easily recognize My voice. I convict, but I'll never condemn. I ask you to obey, but I never demand obedience of you. I rejoice over you. I declare that you are accepted, forgiven, loved, and redeemed. I have so much to say to you. The indwelling Holy Spirit assists you in prayer and intercedes on your behalf in accordance with My will. He encourages you, empowers you, and gives you hope.

Sweet Holy Spirit, I am ready to listen. Lead me into Your presence and speak Your loving thoughts over me that I may live out of who You say I am.

*As God's chosen people, holy and dearly loved,
clothe yourselves with compassion, kindness,
humility, gentleness and patience.*

COLOSSIANS 3:12

I OPPOSE THE PROUD, but show favor to the humble.
When you come to Me cloaked in humility and kindness,
I show you favor. As My Spirit fills you, you take on My
attitudes and likeness. Let Him express My love through
you. It's impossible for you to imitate Me without abiding
in the Spirit. You are empowered to live a supernatural
life above the fray of this world through His indwelling
presence—a life marked by grace, whereby you extend
compassion and kindheartedness to the hurting and gentleness and patience to the vulnerable. When you walk in
humility, you are as alluring as honey is to a bee. You are
a light shining in the darkness for Me.

*Spirit of God, clothe me with Your compassion, kind-
ness, humility, gentleness, and patience. Let me shine
Your light in the darkness as You love people through
me.*

205

JULY 15

The Lord is good, a refuge in times of trouble.
He cares for those who trust in him.

NAHUM 1:7

I AM YOUR REFUGE. I know it feels overwhelming for you to live in this world at times. When you experience heartbreak and loss, suffering and pain, and tests and trials, your natural tendency is either to isolate or lash out. I see you, and I wait for you to turn to Me. The Spirit produces peace and draws you into intimacy with Me—you are not alone. I use each situation for good, and if you allow Me, I make beauty from ashes. I keep track of all your sorrows and collect all your tears. I hold you close until the pain begins to fade and you are able to catch your breath. I lavish you with hope and grace, and when you are ready, I help you stand again. I am good, and I care for you.

Spirit of God, flood me with perfect peace and sustain me when it feels like my world is crumbling. You are my refuge, and I trust You to use my pain and disappointment to draw me into deeper intimacy with You.

JULY 16

"For my thoughts are not your thoughts, neither are your ways my ways," declares the Lord. *"As the heavens are higher than the earth, so are my ways higher than your ways and my thoughts than your thoughts."*

ISAIAH 55:8–9

DON'T BE SURPRISED to find yourself in a position you never thought you would find yourself—a situation that seems unimportant, less than desirable, mundane, chaotic, or even scary. I will lead you to places that make no natural sense in order to supernaturally accomplish My plan and purpose. Most of the time, My will is not linear. Instead, I am preparing the way for something you cannot conceive in the future. I know the past, present, and future. All things are under My control, and My Spirit will always be with you on your journey. Trust Me to work everything out in My way and in My timing. I am writing the story of your life. It will be full of unexpected twists and turns—and it will have the perfect ending.

Heavenly Father, help me to see the story You are writing in my life as an adventure. Thank You for giving me Your Spirit to lead me on my journey.

I have hidden your word in my heart that
I might not sin against you.

PSALM 119:11

MY WORD IS PREVENTATIVE MEDICINE for your soul. Sin always causes death—the death of a relationship, the death of a dream, the death of hope. But I am life-giving. My mercy and grace break the chains of bondage as I wash you white as snow with My forgiveness. My mercies are new every morning, giving you a clean slate and a fresh start. I lift the heavy burden of sin as the Spirit leads you into freedom. Meditating on My Word is like taking a daily dose of vitamins to build your immune system. When you plant My Word deep in your heart, it sows My truth in you, helping you to resist temptation. Delight in My Word, feast on My truth, and My Spirit will satisfy your soul.

Heavenly Father, I praise You for the gift of Your life-giving Word. Implant Your truth deep in my heart for me to draw on often. Thank You for Your gracious forgiveness and the opportunity to begin each day with a fresh start.

There is no fear in love.
But perfect love drives out fear . . .

1 JOHN 4:18

BRING ALL OF YOUR FEARS TO ME. When you feel fear begin to well up inside you, begin a conversation with My Spirit living inside you. He will guide you out of fear and into My perfect peace. Your fear comes from feeling unsure, unsafe, and vulnerable. As you relinquish your anxiety and fear to the Spirit, He will exchange it for My hope and peace. You tend to turn to your coping mechanisms when anxiety begins to creep in—food, alcohol, nicotine, drugs shopping, sex, pornography—but they only offer momentary relief. I am your anchor of peace! When life feels out of control, tether yourself to Me. Call on the Spirit to hem you in with My perfect, unconditional, unchanging, everlasting love. My love casts out all fear, and because you are My child, you can never stray outside of My love. I am your safety net. You are secure in Me.

Heavenly Father, I want to keep in step with Your Spirit moment by moment during my day, but I am inclined to take the wheel and try to control people and outcomes. Help me to trust You with everything that is going on in my life.

You have not received a spirit that makes you fearful slaves. Instead, you received God's Spirit when he adopted you as his own children.

ROMANS 8:15, NLT

BRING ALL OF YOUR FEARS TO ME. I want to replace your fear with My perfect peace. Your fear comes from feeling unsure, unsafe, and vulnerable. Relinquish your anxiety and fear to the Spirit, and He will exchange it for My hope and peace. I am safe and offer security. When life feels out of control, I am your anchor of peace. I love you with a perfect, unconditional, everlasting love. A child of Mine can never stray outside of My love. My love casts out all fear. My beloved child, you are safe and secure in My presence.

Heavenly Father, I am Your child, and I anchor my life to You. Help me to recognize the warning signs when fear and anxiety begin to creep in so I can invite the Spirit to exchange them for Your perfect peace.

Make every effort to keep the unity
of the Spirit through the bond of peace.

EPHESIANS 4:3

SPENDING TIME ALONE WITH ME will allow you to make peace with yourself and peace with others. You are My instrument of peace to the broken, the hurting, and the divided. Many of My precious children have become intolerant, opinionated, and prejudiced. Spend time with Me and learn how to relate to others with My love. Rely on the Spirit to facilitate peace when emotions flare. If you keep your mind steadfast on Me, I will keep you in perfect peace.

Heavenly Father, grow in me a heart of love and com-
passion to love those You love. Teach me to be a peace-
maker and a uniter as I point people to You.

Devote yourselves to prayer,
being watchful and thankful.

COLOSSIANS 4:2

THE GOAL OF PRAYER IS TO CONNECT WITH ME. Pull away and sit quietly with Me. Simply be still in My presence. One of the most intimate ways you can develop your relationship with Me is to spend time with Me with no agenda. Unhurried time spent with Me will soothe your spirit and eliminate distractions that prevent you from hearing My voice. The Spirit reveals Me to you and speaks to your heart during prayer. Even as you move through your day, maintain sweet communion with Me by remaining conscious of My presence.

Heavenly Father, I want to grow in my ability to hear You and what You have to say to me personally. Help me to discipline myself to pull away and spend unhurried time with You.

My people have done two evils:
They have turned away from me,
the spring of living water.
And they have dug their own wells,
which are broken wells that cannot hold water.

JEREMIAH 2:13, NCV

YOU WERE MADE FOR ME, and I know what you need. There's a void in you that only I can fill. I created you and know what satisfies you. You will be tempted to place your happiness and your hope in people, money, and pleasure. These are manmade wells that will only temporarily satisfy. My water is fresh and gushes forth; it does not grow stale and never runs dry. Come to Me. Saturate yourself in My life-giving presence. Allow My Spirit to reveal your desperate need for Me. Bring all of yourself to Me—your sorrows and burdens along with your joys and desires—and I will give you what you need.

Holy Spirit, help me to sit in the stillness of Your presence and drink from Your eternal fountain of fresh, thirst-quenching, living water. Forgive me for searching for satisfaction in all the wrong places when You alone satisfy my soul. You are enough.

In the same way,
the Spirit helps us in our weakness.

ROMANS 8:26

I AM YOUR COMFORTER and closest companion. Come to Me with all your weaknesses. I am aware of all that you deal with—physical pain, emotional pain, financial stress, or personal problems. The Spirit helps, comforts, and counsels you. My strength provides peace of mind. When doubt, fear, worry, or anxiety flood your thoughts, focus on My security rather than your insecurities. Cry out for help when you are overwhelmed, and I will rescue you. In your weakness, I am strong.

Heavenly Father, remind me that You are bigger than any of my weaknesses. Thank You for Your presence, power, and fellowship. You are my safe haven.

Though the fig tree does not bud and there
are no grapes on the vines, though the olive crop fails
and the fields produce no food, though there are no sheep
in the pen and no cattle in the stalls, yet I will rejoice
in the LORD, I will be joyful in God my Savior.

HABAKKUK 3:17–18

I LONG TO BE BY YOUR SIDE during the difficult seasons of your life. Your struggles do not have to be unbearable. Don't miss what I am doing during tough times. My Spirit gives you peace in the midst of difficulty and helps you carry the weight of your burdens. Basing your joy on circumstances causes you to second-guess Me and battle deep frustration. You are an overcomer by the power of the Spirit. I am always by your side. Sit with Me during stressful circumstances and delight yourself in My presence. Rejoice in Me! I strengthen you to persevere through what you face and find joy in your journey.

Spirit of God, give me a heart of praise during difficult seasons. Help me to seek You and find You, and empower me to trust in the midst of pain and struggle.

For the mind set on the flesh is death,
but the mind set on the Spirit is life and peace.

ROMANS 8:6, NASB

OPEN YOURSELF TO MY SPIRIT, and I will reward you with the peace you seek. It is futile to strive for peace on your own. When your mind wanders and your thoughts are absent of Me, life will only become more chaotic. Begin your day with a conscious awareness of the Spirit, and recognize My radiant presence throughout your day. The Spirit will live through you and guide you to a life of serenity.

Heavenly Father, empower me to walk by Your Spirit each day so I may experience Your peace and be a peacemaker for You.

Because you are my help, I sing in the shadow of your wings. I cling to you; your right hand upholds me.

PSALM 63:7–8

THE SAFEST PLACE FOR YOU is in the shadow of My wings. I am your hiding place and help. My loving-kindness and compassion are a shield from the weariness that chases you. Rest in My faithfulness. My Spirit upholds you and covers you in peace. I will never leave you; I will never let you down. My love never fails and never gives up on you.

Heavenly Father, help me to run to the shadow of Your wings when my world falls apart. I take refuge in You and cling to Your peace and protection.

*When God our Savior revealed his kindness
and love, he saved us, not because of the
righteous things we had done, but because of his mercy.
He washed away our sins, giving us a new birth
and new life through the Holy Spirit.*

TITUS 3:4–5, NLT

GIVE ALL OF YOURSELF TO ME. I rescued you. You are no longer a slave to sin and death. Because of My great love and mercy, I saved you and made you My heir. My prevailing grace and the work of My Spirit made you new—with new thoughts, desires, and affections. You are a new creation in Christ. My work in you is inward and spiritual. Walk in faith, knowing that I have restored My relationship with you now and for eternity.

Heavenly Father, make me into Your likeness and the image of Jesus Christ. Teach me to live out of the new life You have given me instead of floundering in my flesh.

Be very careful, then,
how you live—not as unwise but as wise,
making the most of every opportunity,
because the days are evil.

EPHESIANS 5:15–16

SEEK ME for daily wisdom. Time is your most valuable commodity. Spending unhurried time with Me is the best use of your time—it increases your discernment to live wisely. You live in a culture pushing you to act as though there is never enough time, constantly rushing and never slowing down. There is a temptation to make every moment of time connected and productive. Time is a gift from Me, so seek Me on how to use it wisely. I will supply you with wisdom to live each day effectively by the power of My Holy Spirit.

Heavenly Father, help me to use my time wisely in order to leave a mark on this world for You. Help me to make the most of the time and opportunities You give me.

God has given us his Spirit
as proof that we live in him and he in us.

1 JOHN 4:13, NLT

YOU ARE COMPLETELY SECURE in our relationship. I deposited My Spirit in you, and He is a sign of your true faith. The Spirit is like a down payment—the assurance that we will spend eternity together. He is your Helper and enables you to remain under My influence. Because of the work of the Spirit, you abide in Me, and I abide in you, creating sweet communion between us. The Spirit within you assures you with absolute certainty that you are My child.

Spirit of God, thank You for the gift of the Spirit to help me live a life pleasing to You. He gives me complete assurance that I am Your child.

May the God of hope fill you with all joy
and peace as you trust in him, so that you may overflow
with hope by the power of the Holy Spirit.

ROMANS 15:13

I AM YOUR HOPE. You live in a fallen world, and in this world you will have trouble. You will experience disappointments, heartbreak, and many setbacks. Run to Me as your source of hope in the midst of your trials and suffering. My hope is not simply a positive outlook that everything will work out for you. The basis for My hope is in the power of My Holy Spirit and the assurance that I will keep all My promises. The Spirit produces an enduring joy and peace in you that overflows for the watching world to see.

Heavenly Father, help me to endure tribulations knowing that they are temporary and something greater awaits me in eternity. You are my only hope. Fill me with joy and peace as I trust You.

Do you not know that your bodies are temples of the Holy Spirit, who is in you, whom you have received from God? You are not your own; you were bought at a price. Therefore honor God with your bodies.

1 CORINTHIANS 6:19–20

YOU ARE VALUABLE. I chose you to be the dwelling place of My Spirit, and I have taken up permanent residence in your heart. You have great value in My eyes. I have set you apart and paid the ultimate price for you. I am with you wherever you go, and I am a part of whatever you do. I want to use you for My purposes, so yield to Me and honor Me with your body. As you daily surrender to Me, the Spirit gives you the power and strength to keep yourself sacred for My use.

Spirit of God, breathe on me and empower me to live a life worthy of Your calling. By Your power, I can exercise self-control to live for Your glory and service.

AUGUST

*The Spirit himself
testifies with our spirit
that we are God's children.*

ROMANS 8:16

On the last and greatest day of the festival, Jesus stood and said in a loud voice, "Let anyone who is thirsty come to me and drink. Whoever believes in me, as Scripture has said, rivers of living water will flow from within them." By this he meant the Spirit.

JOHN 7:37–39

YOU WERE CREATED with an insatiable thirst in your soul that I alone can quench. I am your source of fulfillment, and the Spirit satisfies your soul with never-ending rivers of living water. Because of your faith in Me, the Spirit lives in you. The presence, power, and companionship of My Spirit is a free gift to you. You spend so much time searching for satisfaction in what you do, what you have, how you look, approval from people—and none of that fulfills you. When you feel the temptation to look for satisfaction and purpose outside of Me, stop and drink from My river of living water within you.

Spirit of God, thank You for creating in me a thirst that only You can satisfy and for supplying me with an unending supply of living water to quench my dehydrated heart. Fill me to overflowing with Your living water and let others see how satisfying You are.

AUGUST 2

*I tell you the truth: it is to your advantage that I go away,
for if I do not go away, the Helper will not come to you.
But if I go, I will send him to you.*

JOHN 16:7, ESV

THE SPIRIT IS A GIFT TO YOU. He is in you and with
you—you are never alone. He is your Helper; simply
reach out and ask Him for help. You will face problems,
difficulties, and hardships, but you will never be alone in
the battle. The Spirit is your Helper, Comforter, Advocate,
Counselor, and Strengthener. He empowers you to handle any challenge you face. Take advantage of the power
I deposited in you. My Spirit is ever-present—in all places
at all times—to walk with you on your journey.

*Holy Spirit, help me to truly believe You are with me
every step of the way. Thank You for watching and
waiting for me. Empower me to overcome any temptation or difficulty I face.*

Where can I go from your Spirit?
Where can I flee from your presence? If I go up to the
heavens, you are there; if I make my bed in the depths,
you are there. If I rise on the wings of the dawn,
if I settle on the far side of the sea, even there your
hand will guide me, your right hand will hold me fast.

PSALM 139:7-10

SOMETIMES YOU WANT TO RUN AND HIDE FROM ME because you feel unworthy to be in My presence because of your guilt and shame. There is no need to hide from Me. I don't condemn you—I forgive you. There is no sin too great that can keep you from My redeeming love. That's why it's called amazing grace! My Son demonstrated the ultimate example of love and forgiveness when He chose to be the substitute for your sin. Because of His sacrifice, there is nothing that can separate you from My presence—nothing. My Spirit lives within you, and He is always with you. My compassion never fails. My love is enduring. I will always pursue an intimate relationship with you. You are perfectly known and loved in every way.

Spirit of God, You are faithful. Guide me and keep me
from stumbling. I am grateful there is nothing I can do
that will separate me from You.

Be strong in the Lord and in his mighty power.
Put on the full armor of God,
so that you can take your stand against the devil's
schemes. Take the helmet of salvation and the
sword of the Spirit, which is the word of God.

EPHESIANS 6:10–11, 17

BE ARMED AND READY to take on the challenges of your day. Meet Me on a regular basis and spend time with Me in My Word. You were created to have fellowship with Me—your devotional life is vital to your spiritual life. Don't make the tragic mistake of spending your entire life neglecting Me, only to later realize the treasured time we missed together. Too many of My children are underfed on My Word and live defeated lives. Growing in your faith and becoming a mature disciple is a part of My plan for you. You have My Word, the Holy Spirit, and prayer to teach and equip you.

Heavenly Father, I sincerely want to grow closer to You and spend time with You. Awaken in me a passion for Your Word and help me develop a habit of spending time in Your presence.

Yet a time is coming and has now come
when the true worshipers will worship the Father
in the Spirit and in truth, for they are the kind of
worshipers the Father seeks. God is spirit, and his
worshipers must worship in the Spirit and in truth.

JOHN 4:23-24

WORSHIP ME IN SPIRIT AND TRUTH. Worship is internal and far more than an outward ritual. Worship is an attitude of the heart. Jesus ushered in an entirely new way of worship—not dependent on place but on your attitude. I love your heartfelt expression of adoration for Me. My Spirit leads you into My presence through worship, where I can tend to the tender places in your heart and you can experience Me for who I really am. Come to Me and worship.

Heavenly Father, I adore You. Create in me a heart so enamored by You that it moves me to worship You in Spirit and truth.

Do not quench the Spirit.

1 THESSALONIANS 5:19

YIELD TO ME and My promptings so you won't quench the Spirit. Resisting what I want to do in you or through you can stifle the Spirit within you. Our relationship will blossom when you wait on Me and allow Me to lead and guide you. As you follow My promptings, you will see that you can trust Me and the plan I have for you. I only want what's best for you.

Heavenly Father, I don't want to extinguish Your Spirit. I need Your help. I yearn to follow Your lead in all areas of my life and to say yes to whatever You ask of me.

Hope does not put us to shame,
because God's love has been poured out into our hearts
through the Holy Spirit, who has been given to us.

ROMANS 5:5

STAND UNDER MY GREAT WATERFALL OF LOVE for you, and let it wash over you. Your heart is an acceptance magnet—it moves toward what it regards as attractive or satisfying. Nothing is more satisfying than experiencing My love on a deep, intimate, and personal level. I want to deepen your understanding of My love for you. Each day, ask the Spirit to increase your love for Me and to increase your awareness of My overwhelming love for you. The depth of My love cannot be explained—it can only be experienced. Hope in Me and experience My lavish love.

Heavenly Father, I receive Your lavish love. Help my love for You to increase each day, and use me to love others so they may experience the depth of Your love.

I will give you a new heart and put a new spirit in you; I will remove from you your heart of stone and give you a heart of flesh. And I will put my Spirit in you and move you to follow my decrees and be careful to keep my laws.

EZEKIEL 36:26–27

I AM CREATING SOMETHING NEW IN YOU. I gave you a brand-new heart and a new spirit to help you follow Me. My Spirit enables you to accomplish what is impossible on your own—to joyfully obey My commands. I provide a way to live a life of love and obedience through the power of My Spirit. You will experience great joy and fulfillment when you follow Me.

Heavenly Father, I want to experience great joy and fulfillment from following You. Make me more sensitive to Your Spirit so I can follow You more closely.

The Kingdom of God is not a matter of what we eat or drink, but of living a life of goodness and peace and joy in the Holy Spirit.

ROMANS 14:17, NLT

RULES AND REGULATIONS CAN TRIP YOU UP spiritually. You can get wrapped up in My law and miss the point of My grace. Obedience is important to Me, but My grace covers your sin and failures. I gave what is most valuable to Me—My Son's life—in order to maintain a permanent relationship with you. My kingdom isn't about power and performance. My kingdom is about living in the power of the Spirit. Don't waste another moment living in the bondage of legalism. Instead, allow the Spirit to radically empower you to live a life of goodness and peace and joy.

Spirit of the Living God, fall fresh on me and fill my life with great joy!

Faith is the assurance of things hoped for,
the conviction of things not seen.

HEBREWS 11:1, ESV

WHEN THINGS DON'T GO YOUR WAY, trust My way.
Most of the time you can't see the outcome of what I am
doing. Some realities are unseen because they are so far
in the future—and future things belong to Me alone. I
know there are times when your circumstances feel too
difficult, and you lose all hope. Wait on Me. Place your
hope in Me because I am working all things for good. Ask
the Spirit for an eternal perspective—ask Him to reveal
things in the spiritual realm because things aren't always
as they appear. Trust Me as you wait on Me for things to
be fulfilled in their appointed time.

Heavenly Father, help me to put my faith and hope in
You alone and trust You with my future.

Blessed is the one who trusts in the LORD,
whose confidence is in him.

JEREMIAH 17:7

BE CONFIDENT IN WHO YOU ARE because of who I am. Your confidence comes from knowing Me. As you spend time in My presence, the Spirit reveals to you who I am and who you are. Your identity does not depend on what people think about you. Your identity does not depend on what you own. Your identity does not depend on what you accomplish. You are who you are because of who I say you are. You are no longer a slave, but a child and an heir. You are a new creature in Christ—redeemed and forgiven. You are chosen, holy, and blameless. I love you and chose you. You are My child.

Heavenly Father, open the eyes of my heart that I may be fully alive to my true identity. Teach me to see myself as You see me. Thank You for the new identity I have in You.

The LORD will fulfill his purpose for me.
LORD, your faithful love endures forever;
do not abandon the work of your hands.

PSALM 138:8, CSB

I CREATED YOU TO ENJOY A RELATIONSHIP WITH ME and to live out My purpose for you. Everything I create has a purpose. As My child, I long for you to have great clarity and know your purpose. I am aware of the angst and frustration you experience when you are unaware of your purpose. I provide perfect peace when you trust the Spirit to lead and guide you. He is your internal compass—like a navigation system—and will give you direction. Stay in constant communion with the Spirit and allow Him to guide you. Fulfilling My mission for you is an essential part of abundant living.

Heavenly Father, show me my purpose and give me the courage to follow wherever You lead. Grant me the joy of Your presence and the pleasure of following You forever.

You will keep in perfect peace those whose minds
are steadfast, because they trust in you.

ISAIAH 26:3

FIX YOUR THOUGHTS ON ME to remain in perfect peace. All you have to do is ask the Spirit to give you a conscious awareness of Me throughout your day. You fear you won't get what you want unless you control everything around you, but true peace comes from the assurance that I am fully in control. I know you intimately and am involved with every detail of your life. Don't allow the noise of life—chatter, people, and irrelevant details—to distract you from keeping your mind steadfast on Me and experiencing My peace.

Heavenly Father, shower my soul with Your peace so that I may be free from all anxiety and worry. Ease my racing heart and quiet my mind as I trust You with my entire life.

The Lord replied, "My Presence will go with you,
and I will give you rest."

EXODUS 33:14

MY PRESENCE IS WITH YOU throughout your day and calms your soul. Stress, worry, and anxiety are created when you run ahead of Me. Apart from Me, you can do nothing. Dialogue with the Spirit and allow Him to guide you. Stop striving to please everyone. You find rest by completely trusting in Me. When you feel overwhelmed or anxious, focus on Me. Enter into My rest, knowing I am with you and give you everything you need.

Heavenly Father, I can do nothing apart from You. Thank You for always being with me. Help me to live in constant dependence on You and to be fully aware of Your presence. Teach me to rest in You.

*When the Spirit of truth comes, he will guide you
into all the truth, for he will not speak on his own authority,
but whatever he hears he will speak, and he will declare
to you the things that are to come.*

JOHN 16:13, ESV

BE WILLING TO FOLLOW as the Spirit guides you into the fullness of truth. There is so much noise that can distract and misdirect you, but I always lead you in the right direction. Seek Me when you face decisions and life choices, and My Spirit will guide you. You are not alone. I am your safeguard. Bring your burdens to Me, and let Me carry them for you. You are part of a story that is so much bigger than you, and I see the entirety of it. I am intimately involved in every aspect of your life and want to lead, guide, and protect you each step of the way through the power of My Spirit.

Heavenly Father, guide me in truth as I trust You with my future today and every day. Strengthen my faith as I learn to wholly depend on You.

Since you have heard about Jesus and have learned the truth that comes from him, throw off your old sinful nature and your former way of life, which is corrupted by lust and deception. Instead, let the Spirit renew your thoughts and attitudes.

EPHESIANS 4:21–23, NLT

RISE ABOVE NEGATIVE THINKING, which so easily entangles you. Your thoughts determine your behavior and can so easily cause chaos and confusion. When your mind begins to wander toward negativity, bad attitudes, or deceitfulness, ask the Spirit to refocus your thoughts on Me. Ask Him to redirect and control your thoughts. My best work in you is the renewing of your mind. You can't change yourself, but I can transform you from the inside out. I will empower you to let go of old attitudes, thought patterns, and images that you rehearse in your head and replace them with My thoughts and attitudes. I want to free you from the bondage of your old life and lead you to an abundant life full of meaning, hope, and joy.

Spirit of the Living God, transform me by the renewing of my mind. Empower me to live a righteous and holy life so that I will be a sweet aroma to those around me and give You all the glory.

For everything there is a season,
a time for every activity under heaven.

ECCLESIASTES 3:1, NLT

I AM IN CONTROL OF EVERY SEASON of your life. Each season has a purpose. I am always with you, and I will carry you through your most dark, difficult, and dry seasons. Tune out the voice of the Enemy and his lies that nothing will ever change, at least not for you. When you are downcast and weary, spend time with Me and rely on My Spirit to encourage you. I will comfort you and give you hope. Rehearse My past faithfulness and meditate on the truth of who I am. Your life is in My hands, and I arrange even the smallest details and circumstances. I will empower you to persevere and give you patience to endure when you are not sure that you can forge ahead. I am your hope in the darkness and will lead you into a new season. I love you with an everlasting love.

Holy Spirit, give me strength to rely on You when I come to the end of myself. When my world crumbles, help me to cling to hope in You. Teach me to recognize the lies I believe and to know Your voice, which will guide me out of the darkness.

It is the LORD who goes before you.
He will be with you;
he will not leave you or forsake you.
Do not fear or be dismayed.

DEUTERONOMY 31:8, ESV

I AM WITH YOU—yesterday, today, and tomorrow. No matter what you face today, you won't face it alone. Trust Me even when circumstances appear hopeless. When you feel like you are drowning in difficulty, I will pull you out and save you. When you walk through the fire, I will not let you be burned. I go before you and prepare a way for you. Come to Me when you feel alone, tired, and anxious. My Spirit replaces your fear with security and hope. Nothing happens to you that doesn't pass through My hand. I am in control. I strengthen you, I help you, and I uphold you with My righteous right hand. My presence is the key to your courage.

Heavenly Father, thank You for always being with me. Help me to live confidently and securely, knowing You will never leave me or forsake me. When I begin to sink in fear, remind me to rely on the Spirit to replace my fear with hope in You.

I pray that out of his glorious riches he may
strengthen you with power through his Spirit
in your inner being, so that Christ may dwell in your
hearts through faith. And I pray that you, being rooted
and established in love, may have power, together with
all the Lord's holy people, to grasp how wide and long
and high and deep is the love of Christ.

EPHESIANS 3:16–18

COME TO ME in the calm solitude of the morning. Spend unhurried time in My presence. Before the demands of your day bombard you, ask the Spirit to empower and strengthen you inwardly. Your strength will come from time spent with Me as your faith continues to grow. You will be tempted to look for love and acceptance in temporal things, but I will root, ground, and firmly establish you in My everlasting love. The more acquainted you become with the depth and breadth of My love, the better you will be able to love those whom I place in your path. You are secure in My deep, satisfying, unconditional love.

Heavenly Father, renew my strength and fill me with Your power to live victoriously through each day. Help me to comprehend and experience Your amazing grace and love today.

The one who has fashioned us for this very purpose
is God, who has given us the Spirit as a deposit,
guaranteeing what is to come.

2 CORINTHIANS 5:5

I PREPARE A PLACE FOR YOU beyond your wildest imagination. I see how you are weighed down and oppressed by the things of this world. I see you searching for happiness in the comforts of this life and trying to escape your troubles. Take heart—you were not created for this world. This life is momentary—like a mist that quickly evaporates. Our relationship begins on earth, but it continues throughout eternity. I purchased you when Christ died for your sins, and the Spirit in you is like a lifetime warranty—My assurance and promise that guarantees we will spend eternity together. Don't get attached to the things of this earth, for you weren't meant to live here forever. Begin each day praising Me, anticipating that you are one day closer to home.

I praise You, Holy Spirit, and thank You for being my pledge—guaranteeing my hope in Christ and my future to live for all eternity with You. Help me to release my hold on the seen things of this world as I reach for You.

May these words of my mouth and this
meditation of my heart be pleasing in your sight,
Lord, my Rock and my Redeemer.

PSALM 19:14

WATCH YOUR WORDS and use them wisely. Words carry great power. I know their power—I spoke the very world into existence and created the heavens and earth with My words. Each and every person you come into contact with today is made in My image. Choose your words carefully to honor those made in My likeness. Your encouraging, positive, and uplifting words will be refreshing—like a cold drink of water on a hot and humid day—and can soothe someone's soul. Critical, negative, untrue, and judgmental words will burn like scalding hot water and leave a permanent scar when they land on a person's heart. Self-control is a fruit of the Spirit. Ask the Spirit to fill you and empower you to speak life-giving words.

Heavenly Father, I give You control over my words.
I pray that the words of my mouth would honor and
encourage each person I interact with today. When I
am on the brink of speaking words that don't honor
others, prompt me to speak life-giving words that come
from Your Spirit.

The one who keeps God's commands lives in him,
and he in them. And this is how we know that
he lives in us: We know it by the Spirit he gave us.

1 JOHN 3:24

YOUR OBEDIENCE IS EVIDENCE My Spirit lives in you.
I will empower you to pattern your life after Me so that
My commandments won't be a burden on you. I am well
pleased when your actions and attitudes reflect My character because you are allowing the power of the Spirit to
work in and through you. Free yourself from the pressure
of trying so hard to please Me. Instead, ask the Spirit to
direct your path and lead you throughout your day. The
Spirit will empower you to love the unlovable and serve
the demanding, and by this, everyone will know that you
are My child.

Heavenly Father, I am so grateful for the gift of the
Holy Spirit. There is absolutely no way I can live a life
like Christ without the Spirit's empowerment. Teach
me to completely surrender to You all that I am so that
I may walk in Your freedom. Allow me the privilege of
demonstrating Your power to those around me.

Teach me to do your will, for you are my God;
may your good Spirit lead me on level ground.

PSALM 143:10

I WILL TEACH YOU TO DO MY WILL. Turn to Me when you are unsure of what to do. The more you listen to Me, the easier it will be for you to recognize My voice. I am gentle and kind, and My Spirit will lead you in My ways. When darkness and confusion overcome you, don't allow fear to paralyze you. Look not to yourself or others to guide you, but allow the Spirit to direct you down a path that I will make clear. I am faithful and righteous. I am with you always, and I am good.

Heavenly Father, You are good. Thank You for hearing my cries to You, whether they are cries of despair and hopelessness or cries for help. Teach me Your ways, that I may learn to walk in Your truth and rely on Your faithfulness in order to please and glorify You.

*Do not fear, for I am with you; do not be dismayed,
for I am your God. I will strengthen you and help you;
I will uphold you with my righteous right hand.*

ISAIAH 41:10

I AM YOUR SHELTER when you are weak, helpless, or hopeless. Come to Me—I comfort the brokenhearted and crushed in spirit. Even if you can't feel My presence, never doubt that I am near to you and working on your behalf. If you dwell on the worst possible outcomes, you will be consumed with worry and fear as you spiral downward into a valley of despair. Choose to fix your thoughts on Me. Ask the Holy Spirit to control your heart and mind and to give you My peace. I delight when the Spirit transforms you and renews your mind in My Word. Surrender your thoughts to Me and trust Me to walk you through whatever comes your way. I am for you.

Heavenly Father, fill me afresh with the wonder of Your love. Give me the strength to trust You in the midst of adversity. I rely completely on You to overcome fear and live in freedom.

*Don't worry about anything but pray
about everything. With thankful hearts offer
up your prayers and requests to God.*

PHILIPPIANS 4:6, CEV

I WILL CALM YOUR ANXIOUS HEART. In this life you can always find something to cause you to worry. The temptation to worry seems to follow you throughout your day. Worry deceives you and tells you that you are in control. But that is only an illusion, beloved child, for I am in control. Ask My indwelling Spirit to control your thoughts and give you My peace. I am always available and invite you to come to Me when you feel anxious and overwhelmed. When you take your eyes off Me and focus on your circumstances, anxiety will knock on the door of your heart. When you trust Me and live by faith, you will experience My peace out of the overflow of a grateful heart. Your mind believes what you tell it. Feed it truth. Feed it faith. Rest in My love.

Holy Spirit, empower me with strength to live by faith and to trust that You are in control of every aspect of my life. Help me to replace worry with prayer and a heart of thanksgiving.

All of us who have had that veil removed
can see and reflect the glory of the Lord. And the Lord—
who is the Spirit—makes us more and more like him as we
are changed into his glorious image.

2 CORINTHIANS 3:18, NLT

EACH DAY IS AN OPPORTUNITY to become more like Me. Respond to everything you encounter during the day as a part of My master plan and an opportunity for you to continue to conform into My image. This isn't possible in your own strength. My character can only be reproduced through My power source—the Holy Spirit. My abiding Spirit is always available to you and will enable you to put My glory on display for everyone around you as you allow Me to lead you. I have made Myself known to you so you can make Me known to the world. The secret is to always remain in My glorious presence.

Heavenly Father, help me to consciously choose each day to become more like You and reflect Your glory. Thank You for not asking me to live in my own strength, but for giving me Your Spirit to empower me to shine Your light in this dark world.

No one can serve two masters. Either you will hate the one and love the other, or you will be devoted to the one and despise the other. You cannot serve both God and money.

LUKE 16:13

YOUR HEART AND YOUR AFFECTION are what I desire most. You strive and work to serve Me, but what I cherish most is your love. The world pulls you with a strong gravitational force toward materialism, status, and power. The multitude of shiny, flashy, bigger, and better objects will leave you feeling empty and discontent. I have so much for you, but you must release your grip on the things to which you hold so tightly and reach for Me. The chief competitor of your affection for Me is money. I created this world, and everything in it is Mine. I have unlimited resources. Trust Me to provide for your needs. As your heart inclines to Me, the attraction of this world will grow dim and lose its sparkle. You are secure in My love and care.

Heavenly Father, teach me to be content with what You give me. Help me to trust You as my provider. My desire is to love You above all else and to serve only one Master.

There is one God and Father of everything. He rules everything and is everywhere and is in everything.

EPHESIANS 4:6, NCV

THE EARTH IS MINE and all that is in it. There is nothing under the sun that is not in My control—rulers, weather, economy, and war. I am the creator of relationships, and I desire for you to experience the peace of living in unity. I see the messy parts of your life. Turmoil and chaos are the result of you trying to control circumstances and people. Allow the Spirit to lead you out of chaos and confusion, and instead, empower you to love the people you try to control. He teaches you how to humbly, gently, and patiently love others. Your love for others demonstrates to a watching world that you are Mine.

Heavenly Father, I have tried to love others in my own strength, but I can't. Empower me through the Spirit to love those I find impossible to love. Forgive me for trying to control everything and everyone in my life. I want to live a life worthy of the calling of being a child of the one true God.

Walk in love, just as Christ also loved you
and gave Himself up for us, an offering and
a sacrifice to God as a fragrant aroma.

EPHESIANS 5:2, NASB

LOVE PEOPLE, NOT THINGS. Keep company with Me to learn a life of love. Love—loving Me, loving yourself, and loving people—is what is most important to Me. Spend unhurried time with Me to gain My perspective on what love really is. My love is extravagant. My love gives rather than takes. My love keeps no record of wrongs. My love never fails. The Spirit fills and empowers you to love with My love—an unconditional and inexhaustible love. Just remember, He produces My love because you can't manufacture My kind of love in your own power. When you feel like you just can't love anymore, you are ready to begin allowing the Spirit to love through you.

Heavenly Father, teach me to walk in Your love and scatter it wherever I go. I admit that I can't love like You, but I ask Your Spirit to love through me in a way that people will recognize it as Your love. Thank You for Your unconditional, extravagant love.

If I speak in the tongues of men or of angels, but do not have love, I am only a resounding gong or a clanging cymbal. If I have the gift of prophecy and can fathom all mysteries and all knowledge, and if I have a faith that can move mountains, but do not have love, I am nothing. If I give all I possess to the poor and give over my body to hardship that I may boast, but do not have love, I gain nothing.

1 CORINTHIANS 13:1–3

DRAW CLOSE TO ME and your ability to love others will increase. You will see what love really looks like. When you spend time with Me, I envelop you in My unfailing love. You will experience My love, and then My Spirit in you will pour out My love onto those around you. People don't want to hear about love, they want to experience love. They need to be loved with an extravagant and radical love—a love that only My Spirit can produce. Every person you come in contact with today needs love.

Heavenly Father, draw me near and give me a close-up look at real love. Wrap me in Your loving care and send me out into the world—not with knowledge, but with the power of Your Spirit to love to those who need You most.

I have refined you, but not as silver is refined.
Rather, I have refined you in the furnace of suffering.

ISAIAH 48:10, NLT

SUFFERING PRODUCES PERSEVERANCE, character, and hope. I see the strain and stress you are experiencing as you are being refined. Your struggles seem unbearable, and you want to give up. Don't give in and don't give up. The Holy Spirit—the Helper—will navigate you through the hardship. No matter what you face today, you will not face it alone. When you are hurting, My Spirit is your comfort. In your discouragement, I am your hope. In your anxiety, My Spirit is your peace. In your weakness, My Spirit is your strength. You will go through the fiery furnace of suffering many times in life, but you will not be consumed.

Holy Spirit, there are times when I am overwhelmed and feel as if I can't go on. I turn to You for hope and comfort. Renew in me the joy of the Lord.

SEPTEMBER

*God has given
us his Spirit as proof
that we live in him
and he in us.*

1 JOHN 4:13, NLT

SEPTEMBER 1

I focus on this one thing: Forgetting the past and looking forward to what lies ahead, I press on to reach the end of the race and receive the heavenly prize for which God, through Christ Jesus, is calling us.

PHILIPPIANS 3:13–14, NLT

I UNIQUELY CREATED YOU, and I have a purpose for you. Your life is like a race—a marathon, not a sprint. The Spirit will coach you through each leg of your race. You will find fulfillment and joy when you live each day with intentionality and choose to live for something bigger than yourself. The best way to prepare is to consistently carve out time for Me. I am your biggest cheerleader! The Spirit will map out your course and give you the strength and perseverance to run the next mile. I will be with you every step of the way.

Heavenly Father, grant me Your power to run my race. Help me to live intentionally and with eternity in mind. Thank You for cheering me on as I keep my eye on the heavenly prize for which I've been called.

My grace is sufficient for you, for my power is made perfect in weakness. Therefore I will boast all the more gladly about my weaknesses, so that Christ's power may rest on me.

2 CORINTHIANS 12:9

I AM DRAWN TO YOUR WEAKNESS. Your weak places are where the Spirit can accomplish His greatest work. He exchanges your weakness for His power. The pressure you feel to perform is off. The only thing you can offer Me is your weakness, and the Spirit can do more through your weakness than your strength. When His power is on display through your weakness, My glory is made known. I created every fiber in you—I knit you together in your mother's womb—and I don't make mistakes.

Heavenly Father, help me to embrace my weaknesses and give You all the glory for being my strength. Thank You for taking away the pressure to perform and for loving me just as I am.

If we live by the Spirit, let us also walk by the Spirit.

GALATIANS 5:25, NASB

I DEPOSITED THE SPIRIT IN YOU to aid you—a permanent, indwelling Helper. Temptation comes at you from all angles and in all shapes and sizes. The Spirit is a guide to help you with the many decisions and choices you make throughout your day to overcome the temptations you encounter. When you walk by the Spirit, you live in His power. He empowers you to walk in My ways rather than carry out the desires of your flesh—the desires of the old you before you were made new in Me. Let the Holy Spirit produce in you a desire for My ways. My way leads you into peace and joy, love and hope, and redemption and rest.

Spirit of the Living God, fall fresh on me—hour by hour and day by day. Help me to continually stay in step with You. Fill me with Your incredible power to walk in Your ways.

*A branch cannot produce fruit if it is severed from the vine,
and you cannot be fruitful unless you remain in me.
Yes, I am the vine; you are the branches. Those who
remain in me, and I in them, will produce much fruit.
For apart from me you can do nothing.*

JOHN 15:4–5, NLT

THERE IS GREAT POWER in staying connected to Me.
Just as a branch can only produce fruit when it's connected to the vine, so it is with you. I don't want you to dry
up and wither and become dead inside. The Spirit will
connect you to Me and revive your spirit. He's just waiting for you to ask for a fresh filling so He can produce love
and joy in you. He will give you peace and patience. He
will make you kind and gentle. He will exhibit goodness,
faithfulness, and self-control in you. An apple tree only
produces apples. An orange tree only grows oranges. A
vineyard only yields grapes. The only way you can produce fruit for Me is by the power of the Spirit.

*Holy Spirit, I acknowledge that I can't produce spiritual fruit in my own strength. Anoint and empower me
to produce a bumper crop of spiritual fruit, all to the
glory of God!*

You are the light that gives light to the world.
Live so that they will see the good things you do
and will praise your Father in heaven.

MATTHEW 5:14,16, NCV

I AM THE POWER SOURCE for your light. The only way for you to produce light is to stay plugged into Me. As you spend time in My radiant presence, your light will begin to glow brighter. Nothing combats darkness like light. A single match, a flashlight, or a light bulb can overtake great darkness, and no amount of darkness can overtake even the smallest light. The world is full of darkness, but your light will shine brightly and bring glory to Me. I want to use you right where you are to shine My light for all around you to see. You will make an impact on lives you aren't even aware are watching you. As you interact with others, remember that just a little match can light up the darkness and make a big difference.

Heavenly Father, give me the courage to be a small light in a dark world. I want You to make a big difference through me.

I cry out to God Most High,
to God who will fulfill his purpose for me.

PSALM 57:2, NLT

HERE'S A SECRET: You cannot discover the reason I created you without having an authentic relationship with Me. I want you to grasp the meaning and purpose of your life, but it's impossible to do so apart from an intimate relationship with Me. I want to show you what I am doing in the world and invite you to join Me in the story I am writing. This is the real reason you are here—to play an extraordinary and unique part in My story. The Spirit will lead you into understanding and help you to see that your purpose is specifically tied to My purpose. And when you are empowered to live out My purpose, you will realize that I can use you anywhere, anytime. All I need is a willing heart.

Heavenly Father, thank You for giving me a purpose much bigger than myself. Enable me to walk out my destiny and to live every day with purpose.

Do not worry about tomorrow,
for tomorrow will worry about itself.
Each day has enough trouble of its own.

MATTHEW 6:34

WORRY WON'T ADD A SINGLE HOUR TO YOUR LIFE.
Do you not know? Have you not heard? Birds don't sow
or reap, and they don't store food in barns—yet I feed
them. The flowers of the field—they do not labor and
spin, yet they are more beautifully dressed than kings and
queens. Are you not much more valuable than they? You
can depend on Me to care for you. I am trustworthy, and
you can trust Me one day at a time. Daily dependency
keeps you close to Me. Worrying about tomorrow prevents you from enjoying Me today. Worry and anxiety
tear you apart, resulting in stress and fear. The solution
to overcoming worry and anxiety lives in you—My Spirit.
He offers comfort and peace. Real, lasting peace is only
available through the Spirit. It's yours for the asking.

Heavenly Father, thank You for the reminder that I
am more valuable than birds and flowers, yet You
attend to their every need. Teach me to rely on Your
power to overcome anxiety and rest in Your peace and
comfort.

You, O God, have tested us;
you have tried us as silver is tried.

PSALM 66:10, ESV

REFINEMENT IS A BEAUTIFUL PROCESS. It's not easy or without pain, but it is worth it. I am intimately aware of the details of your life. When you experience pain, it's often an opportunity to grow. Ask the Holy Spirit to reveal the root of your pain to you. He will lead you to truth and understanding and help make sense of your pain. He will be with you as you move in and out of grief. He will guide you through the refinery with compassion and help you experience My peace. Find hope in My promise to never leave you or forsake you. I am testing you, purifying you, and creating a beauty in you that comes only from refining. You will walk out of the fire with a heart ablaze with passion for Me. My precious child, hold My hand while I make something beautiful in you.

Heavenly Father, I admit it is painful when You refine and prune me, but I want to mature to become like You. I cling to the promise that You walk with me through my trials. Make something beautiful out of me.

May the Lord of peace himself give you peace at all times and in every way. The Lord be with all of you.

2 THESSALONIANS 3:16

I INVITE YOU INTO MY PRESENCE to find peace and rest. Slip away and meet with Me. You accomplish more in a few minutes in My presence than in a full day's work. When your mind continually spins and you find yourself trying to make everything work in your own power, remind yourself who is in control. I am the King of all the earth, and I reign over the nations. I'm seated on My holy throne, yet I am always with you and know all the details about your heart and life. You can trust Me to handle anything that comes at you. The Spirit guides and directs your steps and keeps you in perfect peace when you keep your mind steadfast on Me.

Heavenly Father, forgive me when I try to control things and work everything out my way. When my mind spins out of control, remind me that You are in complete control. Help me to trust You with anything that comes my way so I can live in Your perfect peace.

I pray that out of his glorious riches he may strengthen you with power through his Spirit in your inner being, so that Christ may dwell in your hearts through faith. And I pray that you, being rooted and established in love, may have power, together with all the Lord's holy people, to grasp how wide and long and high and deep is the love of Christ.

EPHESIANS 3:16–18

IF YOU COULD GRASP THE DEPTH OF MY LOVE for you, everything would change. My love is transforming and powerful. It will change the way you think about yourself, others, and Me. I am love, and My Spirit lives within you, which means My love is within you. Only by the power of My Spirit can My love flow out of you—an unshakable and unmovable love that breaks barriers and reaches out to love the unlovable. You are rooted and established in My love—anchored to and nourished by Me. My indwelling Spirit gives you inner strength and makes room for Christ in your heart.

Heavenly Father, help me to grasp the depth of Your love so that I may trust You with all that I am. Transform me with Your love so that I may love others with Your love.

SEPTEMBER 11

God chose the foolish things of the world
to shame the wise; God chose the weak things of the
world to shame the strong. . . . Therefore, as it is written:
"Let him who boasts boast in the Lord."

1 CORINTHIANS 1:27, 31

I HAVE PERFECTLY EQUIPPED YOU for your personal mission. I created you with passion, skills, and talent, but at times you will feel totally unequipped. There will be moments or seasons when you will feel stretched—like your mission is bigger than you. I'm not looking for the most capable or self-sufficient person. I'm looking for someone to demonstrate My glory and make My name great. I am looking for someone willing to use what I have placed in their hand to partner with Me to accomplish the seemingly impossible. I'm looking for someone who is willing to live supernaturally and radically by relying on the power of the Spirit to accomplish My purposes. I am looking for someone who will boast in Me. I am looking for someone like you.

Heavenly Father, I raise my hand and volunteer to be
used by You. Draw me near, show me the way, and
empower me to do what can only be done in Your su-
pernatural power.

*Since we are surrounded by such a great cloud
of witnesses, let us throw off everything that hinders
and the sin that so easily entangles. And let us run with
perseverance the race marked out for us, fixing our eyes
on Jesus, the pioneer and perfecter of faith.*

HEBREWS 12:1–2

I CREATED YOU to live a life of purpose—to live with intentionality. I created you to live for something bigger than yourself. The Spirit instructs and equips you to run your race as you spend consistent time in My Word. The Spirit leads you away from the pitfalls of sin that so easily entangle, and He directs you to signs and mile markers to help you stay the course. You are the only one who can run your race. Instead of chasing someone else or looking at the routes I've mapped out for others, keep your eyes on Me and live out of the power of the Holy Spirit. When you cross your finish line and complete the course, I will be waiting for you with open arms, saying, "Well done, good and faithful servant."

Heavenly Father, coach me through my race and empower me to stay on Your course. I desire to live for something so much bigger than myself. Help me to keep my eyes on You—my prize.

Jesus answered, "It is written:
'Man shall not live on bread alone, but on every
word that comes from the mouth of God.'"

MATTHEW 4:4

COME TO ME TO REFUEL YOUR SOUL as you begin each day. I long to spend time with you before you jump into the demands of your day. My Word is life-giving. Spending unhurried time with Me in My Word will consistently nourish your soul. When you become weary and worn down, I will be waiting for you. There is no better way to start your day. Morning by morning, My Spirit will increase your understanding of Me and My will for your life. I will supply all your needs for each day. I am waiting for you.

Heavenly Father, I am so grateful You patiently wait for me. Nourish my mind with Your truth and refuel my soul with time spent in Your presence.

*Wait patiently for the L*ORD*.*
Be brave and courageous.
*Yes, wait patiently for the L*ORD*.*

PSALM 27:14, NLT

WHILE YOU WAIT, I AM AT WORK. You may not be able to see Me at work—oftentimes I work behind the scenes—but trust that I am working *in* you and *for* you. I work to resolve your difficult situations, to answer your most heartfelt prayers, and to grow your faith in Me. While you wait, I also work in you. My Spirit produces patience in you when you allow the waiting to do its work in you. Have patience to wait *on* Me and patience to wait *with* Me. Trust in Me while you wait. Rely on the Spirit for strength and courage—even in the midst of uncertainty and difficult times—confidently trusting that I will help you.

Heavenly Father, help me to see waiting on You as an opportunity to trust and grow in You. I want to learn to be patient in Your power as I wait while You are working.

My sheep listen to my voice; I know them,
and they follow me. I give them eternal life,
and they shall never perish;
no one will snatch them out of my hand.

JOHN 10:27–28

INTIMACY WITH YOU is one of My greatest desires. I long for a close personal relationship with you where we communicate and connect throughout the day. I am always speaking to you. Ask My Spirit to train your ear to recognize My still, quiet voice. The loudest voices don't always deserve to be heard. Tune your ear to My voice. I speak to you throughout the day through My Word, through nature and creation, through circumstances, and through people. I also speak through the still, quiet voice of My Spirit prompting your consciousness. The way I choose to reveal Myself and speak to you today will be unique to you, but remember, I will never contradict My written Word. I love you deeply, child of Mine. Intimacy with you is the desire of My heart.

Heavenly Father, give me ears to hear and eyes to see in order to be more aware of You. Heighten my consciousness when You prompt me and help me to recognize Your voice when You speak to me.

SEPTEMBER 16

The righteous person may have many troubles,
*but the L*ORD *delivers him from them all.*

PSALM 34:19

NO MATTER WHAT CHALLENGES and difficulties you face, I am able to deliver you from all of them. When you spend time in sacred communion with Me, I establish a genuine trust relationship with you. Your capacity to trust Me is built on knowing Me. Trust is foundational to believing that I able and I am willing. I delivered Daniel in the lion's den, David in his battle against Goliath, and Noah in the flood. You are no different. I preserved these stories to demonstrate My faithfulness to My people. I am the same deliverer for you. As you sit quietly in My presence, reflect on My past faithfulness, trust in My present work in your life, and remember that I am your salvation for eternity.

I praise You, my Deliverer! As I reflect on Your faithfulness, I am overwhelmed with gratitude for You. Fill me with the fresh wonder of Your love and empower me to trust You in the midst of adversity to overcome fear and live in freedom.

The plans of the Lord stand firm forever,
the purposes of his heart through all generations.

PSALM 33:11

MY PLANS FOR YOU ARE GOOD. My very essence is good—nothing bad can come from Me. I uniquely and intentionally created you, and I have a purpose and plan for your life. The Spirit reveals My plans to you in the quiet stillness of our time together. I eagerly await quality time with you so the Spirit can unveil My good character to you. The more time we spend together, the more clearly you will understand My plans and purpose for you. My plans always involve making you more like Me. You are so often looking for a plan for *what* to do, but My plan for you concerns *who* you are. Your character is far more important to Me than what you achieve. When you trust Me to lead you, what you accomplish becomes My responsibility—and I will always accomplish what's best for you.

Heavenly Father, reveal to me the blueprint for my life. Help me to rest in Your plans and accomplish Your will for my life. Most importantly, make me look more like You rather than making me successful by the world's standards.

He says, "Be still, and know that I am God;
I will be exalted among the nations,
I will be exalted in the earth."

PSALM 46:10

I GIVE YOU THE GIFT OF REST. I give you permission—so give yourself permission—to cease from striving and trying to figure everything out. I yearn for you to spend time in sacred communion with Me. Stay in My presence, away from the hurry and flurry of activity all around you. Turn off the world's noise. You run so hard, so fast until you exhaust all of your strength, and there is nowhere to go but where I am. Hear Me whisper the much-needed reminder, *I love you. I am all you need. I am your soul sufficiency. Be still, and know that I am God.* Come and stand in awe of Me, where the supernatural, inner power of the Holy Spirit can work in you. My Spirit is your source of strength. I knew you wouldn't be able to live this life in your own strength, so I sent Him to live it through you.

Heavenly Father, help me to pull away and rest in You. It's exhausting to attempt to live this life in my own effort. Please empower me and fill me to live in Your supernatural strength.

Pray in the Spirit at all times with all kinds of prayers,
asking for everything you need.
To do this you must always be ready and never give up.
Always pray for all God's people.

EPHESIANS 6:18, NCV

PRAYER FOSTERS INTIMACY WITH ME. I cherish time spent with you. I am your companion and friend, so keep a running conversation with Me, sharing anything and everything that's on your heart and mind. I am always listening. This kind of ongoing conversation is what keeps us in close proximity. The Enemy wants you to believe that prayer is some kind of formula with a prescribed process. Prayer is simply communicating with Me. Ask the Spirit to prompt you as you go about your day to chat with Me and include Me in inner conversations you're having with yourself. As you pray, your level of anxiety and stress diminishes. Prayer itself is a way to find peace.

Heavenly Father, nudge my heart and mind to stay in close communication with You during my day. Help me to remember that prayer is about a relationship with You rather than a task I need to complete.

I will ask the Father, and he will give you another
Counselor to be with you forever. He is the Spirit of truth.

JOHN 14:16–17, CSB

WHEN YOU ARE DISCOURAGED and need someone to talk to, the Spirit listens to you and leads you. When the Enemy comes against you with lies, the Spirit of Truth replaces the lies with My truth. The Counselor is dependable, trustworthy, and always on the ready. The more you listen to Him, the easier it is to recognize His voice and follow His leading. You have a choice—you can wander through this life on your own, or call upon your personal guide, the Holy Spirit. Walk with My Spirit as you journey through life; there's no need to walk alone. Live in His strength and power, not your own. There are so many voices proclaiming truth today that can distract and lead you astray, but there is only one voice of truth—the Spirit of Truth. Just call your Counselor, and He will lead you in truth and righteousness.

Heavenly Father, I welcome Your Spirit in my life. Counsel me in truth, lead me into wisdom and understanding, and guide my steps. Prick my conscience when I am being deceived by lies masquerading as truth.

I cry out to God Most High,
to God who fulfills his purpose for me.

PSALM 57:2, ESV

I MADE YOU ON PURPOSE. Knowing your purpose gives your life meaning. My desire is for you to live out of your purpose, which leads you into fulfillment. Everything in your world has an expiration date—the milk in your refrigerator, your car registration, and even your life. "Nothing lasts forever" is a popular expression. Well, nothing on earth lasts forever. But your life is eternal—you will be with Me forever. I want your life to count, for you to live in utter dependence on My Spirit so your life doesn't waste away without meaning. I numbered your days—each one was ordained before you drew your first breath. I long for you to live with the joy of knowing the impact you are making for eternity.

Heavenly Father, reveal my life purpose to me and grant me the joy of living in light of eternity. Use me in whatever way You see fit for Your glory.

Blessed are those who have learned to acclaim you,
*who walk in the light of your presence, L*ORD*.*
They rejoice in your name all day long;
they celebrate your righteousness.

PSALM 89:15–16

MY RADIANCE LIGHTS YOUR PATH as you walk with Me. The Spirit fills you with joy when you celebrate and rejoice in Me throughout your day. Praising Me reminds you of who I am. I am your Savior, Shepherd, Redeemer, Healer, Abba Father. I am your righteousness, peace, provider, and protector. I am the King of kings and the Lord of lords. I am the God who sees you. I am the Lord God Almighty. I am your strength and your defense; I am your salvation. If I am for you, who can be against you? You have nothing to fear. Place all your trust in Me.

Heavenly Father, I give You all honor, glory, and praise. You alone are worthy! May Your Spirit lead me into Your presence throughout the day.

*I no longer call you servants, because a servant
does not know his master's business. Instead,
I have called you friends, for everything that I learned
from my Father I have made known to you.*

JOHN 15:15

I AM YOUR FATHER, CREATOR, REDEEMER, AND LORD, but I am also your friend. A friend loves at all times, and I love you with an everlasting love. As your friend, I long to spend time with you. I desire more than a superficial relationship with you—a relationship where you freely open your heart and share your deepest desires, your darkest secrets, your joys and fears, and your dreams and discontentment with Me. I created you to be My companion, and that kind of relationship is only developed by spending significant time together. My Spirit softens your heart, draws you close, and knits our hearts together when you choose to spend time in My presence. Just as you would pick up the phone and call a friend, call Me to share what you are thinking about, dreaming about, and how you are feeling.

*Heavenly Father, help me to see You as my friend.
Empower me to run to You in authenticity rather than
from You because of shame and guilt.*

If the LORD does not build the house, the work of the builders is useless; if the LORD does not protect the city, it does no good for the sentries to stand guard.

PSALM 127:1, GNT

I AM THE BUILDER OF YOUR LIFE. I see you planning and working and stressing over details and responsibilities that belong to Me. Apart from the Spirit, you work in vain. I did not create you to orchestrate and plan your life, working day and night to accomplish what you set out to achieve, worrying and fretting over things in which you have no control. Quite the opposite! Your instincts propel you into fix-it mode and problem-solving when you face obstacles, trials, difficulties, and setbacks, leaving you exhausted and anxiety-ridden. I long for you to come to Me in these times to share your heart and problems with Me so I can care for you. Ask My Spirit, the Helper, for help! The Spirit works in and through you and leads you to utter dependence on Me—and you can depend on Me.

Heavenly Father, I have tried and failed many times to live in my own effort and strength. It only leads to exhaustion, disappointment, and feelings of failure. Teach me to surrender to You and allow Your Spirit to lead me into the life You have planned for me.

*The Lord is the Spirit, and where the
Spirit of the Lord is, there is freedom.*

2 CORINTHIANS 3:17

THERE ARE SO MANY THINGS that stand in the way of you viewing Me as I am, blocking My glory from your line of sight. Busyness distracts you from Me. Broken relationships cause pain and heartache. Unforgiveness, bitterness, anger, and sin create a barrier between you and Me, but it doesn't have to be that way. My Spirit blows in your life like a fresh wind and blows out the dust and cobwebs of bondage that quietly settle in your heart and replaces them with My freedom. I give you freedom to come to Me just as you are and to see Me in all My glory. My Spirit opens your eyes to who I am—your never-changing, all-powerful, ever-present, merciful, loving heavenly Father. I alone can satisfy you. I alone am worthy of your worship, surrender, and love. It all begins with My Spirit, because where the Spirit of the Lord is, there is freedom.

Heavenly Father, open my eyes to Your character and truth and help me to live in Your freedom. I stand in awe of Your glorious nature and worship You for who You are.

Teach me to do your will, for you are my God;
may your good Spirit lead me on level ground.

PSALM 143:10

I SHOW YOU WHAT TO DO and teach you My ways. When your life is shipwrecked and you are drowning in sorrows, I lead you to safe, level ground. When deep darkness floods your heart, My good Spirit leads you into comfort. When fear and anxiety overwhelm you, My good Spirit leads you into peace. When the ground opens up and grief swallows you, My mercy never fails. My good Spirit not only teaches you My truth, He empowers you to live by My truth. He imparts wisdom and leads you into understanding. Walk in the Spirit, and you will walk securely on level ground.

Heavenly Father, You are good! Lead me onto level ground where You can instruct me in Your ways and empower me to live according to Your ways. Thank You for Your ever-present love and peace.

Your kingdom come, your will be done,
on earth as it is in heaven.

MATTHEW 6:10

THERE IS NO LIMIT to what I can accomplish through you. I chose you as a vessel to further My kingdom on earth as it is in heaven. Ask the Spirit to enlarge your vision about what is possible in My power. My vision for the world is big and bold, and I invite you into My story. The Spirit will empower you along the way as I lead you to people and situations where My grace and mercy is needed. The light of Christ will shine through you when you invest in My eternal endeavors. I love to see you partner with Me in sharing My hope. With the Spirit leading, each day will be an adventure.

Heavenly Father, give me a passion for eternal activities. I ask You to enable me to further Your kingdom on earth as it is in heaven by being bold and courageous for You.

Nor do I count my life dear to myself, so that I may finish my race with joy, and the ministry which I received from the Lord Jesus, to testify to the gospel of the grace of God.

ACTS 20:24, NKJV

I CHOSE YOU and have a specific purpose and calling for your life. Don't allow what others are doing to distract you from your mission. It's wasted energy to compare yourself to others. Instead, call on the Spirit to confirm your identity in Me. Avoid envy's temptation to be someone you are not—I delight in who I made you to be. You are My unique creation, made by Me and for Me. You are Mine, and I love you with a perfect love. I whisper how much I love you when you sit with Me and seek My face.

Heavenly Father, You made me with a unique purpose and calling. Help me to stay focused on my mission and run the race You set before me. Give me the wisdom to be aware of distractions that cause sideways energy. I want to fulfill Your mission and calling for my life.

I pray that out of his glorious riches he may strengthen you with power through his Spirit in your inner being, so that Christ may dwell in your hearts through faith.

EPHESIANS 3:16–17

THE WORK OF THE SPIRIT IN YOUR LIFE is attractive. When you are completely secure in Me, rooted and established in My love, My Spirit produces an inner beauty and strength in you that outshines outward appearance. When you trust the Spirit to lead you, you exhibit a magnetic peace and joy that spills out for others to see and draws them to Me. My presence fills you and provides the strength you need to sustain your faith. My beautiful child, rest in the depth and breadth of My love for you.

Heavenly Father, strengthen me with the power of Your Spirit. Fill me with Your presence so that my inner beauty points people to the wonder and beauty of Your love.

SEPTEMBER 30

*When the Companion comes, whom I will
send from the Father—the Spirit of Truth who
proceeds from the Father—he will testify about me.*

JOHN 15:26, CEB

I LOVE WHEN YOU BRING YOUR QUESTIONS TO ME.
When you have a sense of unrest in your spirit, slow down
and engage in conversation with Me. Listen for the quiet
voice of the Spirit and ask Him to reveal My truth to you. I
know you need reassurance, which is why I sent the Spirit
to live within you. Bring your doubts and questions to Me
to discover My truth and My will. I don't withhold what's
good for you—the Spirit leads you into truth and understanding. He teaches you My ways and how to discern
My voice. Tune your ear to the Spirit's voice, beloved, for
I want the very best for you.

*Heavenly Father, thank You for allowing me to bring
my questions and concerns—my doubts and unbe-
lief—to You without judgment. I need the reassurance
of Your Word and Your presence. Thank You for so
generously giving Your wisdom.*

OCTOBER

Hope does not put us to shame,
because God's love has been poured
out into our hearts through the
Holy Spirit, who has been given to us.

ROMANS 5:5

Teach me to do your will, for you are my God.
May your gracious Spirit lead me forward on a firm footing.

PSALM 143:10, NLT

TRUST ME and the leading of My Spirit. If I quicken your spirit to share the gospel with the nations, then go share the gospel with the nations. If I stir you in prayer to seek forgiveness, then seek forgiveness. If I prompt you while studying My Word to serve the poor, then serve the poor. If the Spirit incites you to wait, then wait. If I nudge you to go, then go. My stirrings, agitations, and promptings of your spirit are for your benefit and protection, so be sensitive to them and follow the Spirit's leading.

Heavenly Father, I trust You and the leading of Your Spirit. Guide me with a sensitive heart into Your perfect will.

OCTOBER 2

Cause me to understand the way of your precepts, that I
may meditate on your wonderful deeds. My soul is weary
with sorrow; strengthen me according to your word.

PSALM 119:27–28

SPENDING TIME IN MY PRESENCE is where you'll find
your strength. Hide My Word in your heart—it nourishes
and prepares you for the day ahead. When you are downcast and lonely, the Spirit overshadows you with peace
and comfort. I created you with a craving that I alone can
satisfy. My Word feeds your hungry soul and nourishes
your spirit. The Spirit sustains and strengthens you according to My Word. He causes you to understand My
ways. Feast on My life-giving Word so that you can be
strong for the battles you will face.

Heavenly Father, I crave Your truth, yet I often feed
myself on the empty offerings of the world. You alone
can satisfy me. Guide me into truth and lead me to
Your life-giving Word.

OCTOBER 3

Nevertheless, with most of them God was not pleased,
for they were overthrown in the wilderness.
Now these things happened as examples for us,
that we might not desire evil as they did.

1 CORINTHIANS 10:5–6, ESV

THE WAYS OF THIS WORLD ARE ENTICING, but they lead to despair and destruction. My ways are contradictory to the ways of the world, and they lead to life and hope. The Spirit uproots your desire for evil ways and plants cravings for My ways in your heart. There is such a strong, magnetic pull to this world and what it offers, but as you walk with Me you find peace and contentment. Reach out and hold My hand to guide you through the tempting pleasures that only lead to emptiness and wanting more. The Spirit empowers you to walk in the light of My Word and rest in My righteousness.

Heavenly Father, uproot my desire for the things of this world and implant cravings for Your ways in my heart so I may rest in Your righteousness.

For by grace you have been saved through faith.
And this is not your own doing; it is the gift of God,
not a result of works, so that no one may boast.

EPHESIANS 2:8–9, ESV

GRACE IS MY GIFT TO YOU. You became My child by grace through faith. In the same way, it is by grace through faith that you mature as My follower. Your flesh tries to flaunt its old habits as teasers for you to not trust Me. But you know better—you know that to boast in the flesh is foolish, but to be humble in the Spirit is wise. When you walk in the Spirit, you are empowered to bear the fruit of the Spirit. I am rich in mercy, and I love you so much that I expressed My kindness to you in Jesus. Beloved, it is by My grace you have been saved.

Heavenly Father, there aren't words enough to express my love and gratitude for Your gift of grace in Jesus. Help me to boast in You alone. I surrender to Your Spirit's power to grow me in Your grace.

*Worship the L*ORD *with gladness;*
come before him with joyful songs.

PSALM 100:2

I AM THE ULTIMATE SOURCE OF JOY. I delight when you come before Me in worship. It's easy for you to focus on serving Me because it's about what you can do for Me. When you worship Me, it honors My greatness and exalts Me above everything. Praising Me is the best way to live because it releases gladness in your heart, which you reflect back to Me—creating a cycle of gratitude and joy in your life. Come to Me in joyful worship and gladness.

Heavenly Father, it's amazing that when I worship You it creates a cycle of gratitude and joy in my life. I want to honor You with my life and my praise.

OCTOBER 6

Understand this, my dear brothers and sisters: You must all be quick to listen, slow to speak, and slow to get angry.

JAMES 1:19, NLT

LIVING IN HARMONY IS A REFLECTION OF ME. I created you for relationships. One of My greatest desires is for you to live in harmony with those around you. The Spirit empowers you to live with restraint, preventing you from reacting emotionally and getting angry. He helps you to listen more than you speak. By His power, you show patience when someone fails to meet your expectations, forgive those who anger you or deeply disappoint you, and love when you are rejected and hated. The Spirit enables you to model the same kind of patience I demonstrate to you.

Heavenly Father, open my ears to listen with patience. Tame my tongue with Your kindness to prevent hurtful words and enable me to forgive when I am hurt. Make me more like You each day.

Those who obey God's commandments remain in fellowship with him, and he with them. And we know he lives in us because the Spirit he gave us lives in us.

1 JOHN 3:24, NLT

SPIRIT-LED LIVING IS ABOUT UTTER DEPENDENCE on Me, not self-reliance. Money, power, and influence are cheap imitations of trust—they are temporal, defenseless, and undependable. Money and status fly away quickly, but My Spirit is permanent and unchanging. The Spirit grows in you an awareness of Me and shows you how to follow Me. Like a hurricane gains strength as time passes, so does My Spirit. Follow Him even when He leads you to places of discomfort. The path leading to utter dependence is littered with trials and tribulation, but it ushers you into sweet fellowship with Me.

Spirit of God, I want to live in Your power. Increase my ability to rely on You, and gently lead me down the path to utter dependence on You.

OCTOBER 8

*If we confess our sins, he is faithful
and just and will forgive us our sins and
purify us from all unrighteousness.*

1 JOHN 1:9

MY LOVE IS INTENTIONAL AND UNCONDITIONAL. I love you unconditionally even when you sin—whether it's intentional or unintentional. Instead of justifying your actions, lean into confession and repentance and accept My grace and forgiveness. My commands are for your protection, not to burden you. Don't be afraid to come to Me with your sin. As far as the east is from the west, so far will I remove your transgressions from you. Walk out of the darkness and run into My forgiveness.

Heavenly Father, I confess my sin and seek Your forgiveness. Thank You for always waiting for me with open arms.

Rejoice always, pray continually, give thanks in all circumstances; for this is God's will for you in Christ Jesus.

1 THESSALONIANS 5:16–18

THERE IS IMMEASURABLE VALUE IN PRAYER. Abiding in Me through prayer and communion keeps us continually connected. Prayer keeps Me in the forefront of your thoughts and opens the channel of communication between us. Give thanks and rejoice in Me. Giving thanks is not dependent on your circumstances—giving thanks is a result of knowing Me. The Spirit enables you to rejoice even in difficult seasons, by producing love, joy, hope, and peace in you. He draws you closer to Me. Pray continually and trust Me to meet all your needs.

Heavenly Father, draw me close to You through prayer and thanksgiving. Strengthen me to not only endure difficult circumstances, but to rejoice and give thanks as I learn to trust You on a deeper level.

Do not be deceived: God cannot be mocked.
A man reaps what he sows.

GALATIANS 6:7

YOUR LIFE CONSISTS OF THE CHOICES YOU MAKE. Stay close to Me, and I will influence your decisions. When you sow obedience, you reap good fruit. When you sow disobedience, you reap bad fruit. My Spirit will empower you to obey My Word, and He will reap a harvest of good fruit through your life. My principle of sowing and reaping is easy to understand when using the example of a farmer. If a farmer sows wheat, then he will harvest wheat. If a farmer sows corn, then he will reap corn. If you abide in Me and stay under the guidance and influence of the Holy Spirit, you will reap eternal fruit.

Heavenly Father, I desire to reap a harvest pleasing to You, but I admit that I can only do so through the power of Your Spirit. Give me the strength to sow eternal fruit.

But if from there you seek the L<small>ORD</small> your God,
you will find him if you seek him with all your heart
and with all your soul.

DEUTERONOMY 4:29

SEEK ME AND YOU WILL FIND ME. Let nothing stifle your search for Me. My heart is drawn to your wholehearted devotion to Me. The Spirit directs your soul in search of Me. When you find Me, you discover My calming presence, My generous acceptance, and My gentle love for you. Keep seeking Me.

Heavenly Father, I seek You with all my heart and all my soul. Help me to find You as You make Yourself known to me.

OCTOBER 12

When he, the Spirit of truth, comes, he will guide you into all the truth. He will not speak on his own; he will speak only what he hears, and he will tell you what is yet to come.

JOHN 16:13

I LONG TO LINGER WITH YOU. My Spirit will provide insight and understanding into confusing circumstances and misunderstandings. He is My secure source of wisdom for you, speaking only what He hears from Me. If you lean into your own understanding, you will remain frustrated; if you follow Me, you will find fulfillment. Trust and obey Me with all your heart, for I have the best way for you.

Heavenly Father, it's so true that I become confused and frustrated when I try to figure things out in my own strength. May Your Spirit lead me with wisdom to trust You and follow You.

Many are the plans in a person's heart,
but it is the LORD's purpose that prevails.

PROVERBS 19:21

COME TO ME IN PRAYER to discern My purpose for you. How will you know if the idea conceived in your heart aligns with My heart? As we spend time together, the Spirit will provide clarity and lead you in My Word to reveal My truth to you. Seek wise counsel to validate the direction I want you to go. Be patient and don't get ahead of Me. My purpose will prevail in time. I am rarely early and never late, so cease striving and be still. My plan will capture your heart and ignite your imagination. Sit calmly in My presence and wait for Me. I promise it will be worth the wait.

Heavenly Father, slow me down and draw me into Your presence. Direct my heart to Your purpose for me. Give me patience to wait on You as You transform me from the inside out.

How sweet are Your words to my taste!
Yes, sweeter than honey to my mouth!

PSALM 119:103, NASB

MY WORDS ARE LIKE HONEY TO YOUR MOUTH. The more intimately you experience Me, the sweeter they taste. I satisfy the longing of your heart when you spend time in My presence. My Spirit empowers you to speak the truth in love and keeps you from delivering harsh and hurtful words. The Spirit softens your speech so you can address difficult issues with grace and a tender heart. As you spend time with Me, I make your words sweet like Mine.

Heavenly Father, let my words speak of Your love and extend to others the grace and mercy You so generously extend to me.

We have been buried with Him through baptism into death,
so that as Christ was raised from the dead through the glory
of the Father, so we too might walk in newness of life.

ROMANS 6:4, NASB

THE SPIRIT EMPOWERS YOU to walk in newness of life. Walk boldly without fear, always relying on your companion. Those who live with an attitude of superiority and hypocrisy miss Me, allowing pride to feed their empty spiritual performance. My desire for you is to surrender into My Spirit's secure rest. He is empowering and life-giving. My yoke is easy, and My burden is light. Stay immersed in My influence and walk with Me in newness of life.

Heavenly Father, thank You for creating new life in me. I surrender to the Spirit so I may walk with You in newness of life.

Jesus looked at him and loved him.
"One thing you lack," he said. "Go, sell everything
you have and give to the poor, and you will have
treasure in heaven. Then come, follow me."

MARK 10:21

WHEN I HAVE ALL OF YOU, YOU LACK NOTHING. Without Me, you lack everything. Money can be the biggest competitor of your affection and the biggest distraction between Me and you. Jesus said it best: "It is more blessed to give than to receive." I love you no matter what, but My heart longs for you to be consumed by Me rather than the stuff of this world. Stuff brings momentary happiness, which quickly fades. I give everlasting and eternal joy. Allow the Spirit to till the soil of your heart with contentment. A life spent in devotion to Me and generous giving is a life of true satisfaction and joy.

Heavenly Father, I surrender all I have to You. I lack nothing if I have You. Help me to be consumed by You rather than the stuff of this world.

OCTOBER 17

The prudent understand where they are going,
but fools deceive themselves.

PROVERBS 14:8, NLT

MY WISDOM PROTECTS YOU from foolish deception and helps you discover My best for you. Relational pain, financial hardships, and emotional pain can be avoided by seeking My wisdom. My ways are not always easy, but they are sure to bring you the most wisdom. Invite My Spirit to guide you in wisdom and to renew your thinking as you walk with Me throughout your day. My wisdom lets you look ahead and spot future pitfalls. I give you everything you need to be wise and prudent. As My follower you have a bonus—the Holy Spirit to give you discernment.

Heavenly Father, I don't want to be a fool, deceiving myself to believe I know what's best for me. Reveal Your ways to me and give me the courage to follow wherever You lead.

*God is so rich in mercy and loves us
with such intense love.*

EPHESIANS 2:4, CJB

MY LOVE IS EXTRAVAGANT. My love and forgiveness give you hope and healing. Like a compassionate father, I see your heart for Me and desire to give you everything you need. I run toward you when you take a step of faith to come back to Me. My Spirit leads you to repentance with kindness, compassion, forgiveness, and a growing relationship with Me. I patiently wait for you to return to My loving embrace. There is nothing that can separate you from My love. Run into My arms of mercy.

Heavenly Father, I have hope because of Your love and forgiveness. Thank You for Your loving patience. Empower me to seek You with my whole heart and live in Your presence.

Suddenly a furious storm came up on the lake, so that the waves swept over the boat. But Jesus was sleeping.

MATTHEW 8:24

THERE IS NO NEED TO PANIC when the circumstances of life swirl around you. What appears to you to be a crisis may be a divine circumstance I orchestrated. I am all-knowing, aware of the past, present, and future. Nothing takes Me by surprise. I hear your prayers when you cry out to Me in search of answers. You look to Me *for* an answer—for knowledge or solutions—rather than looking to Me as *the* answer. If you abide in Me, I will guide you through any situation you face by the power of the Spirit. I love you, dear child, and I will always be your shelter in the storm.

Heavenly Father, remind me when I am searching for answers that You are the answer. Thank You for guiding me through the storms of life. You are my shelter.

Whatever you do, work at it with all your heart, as though
you were working for the Lord and not for people.

COLOSSIANS 3:23, GNT

GIVE YOUR WHOLE HEART TO WHATEVER YOU DO
as though you are working for Me. Labor done for Me
is work you can be proud of regardless of your vocation.
My purpose for work is much more than a paycheck—
it's an opportunity for all who work with you to see My
Spirit at work in you. Your work ethic will intrigue those
around you and make them question the motivation behind your desire to do everything you do with excellence.
This may very well open doors for you to share about Me
that would otherwise be closed. You don't need to be the
very best at what you do, just do your very best for Me.

Heavenly Father, I commit to do my work as though
working for You—with wholehearted effort and excel-
lence. Use the influence You give me to bring others
to Christ.

OCTOBER 21

Let us come boldly to the throne of our gracious God. There we will receive his mercy, and we will find grace to help us when we need it most.

HEBREWS 4:16, NLT

MY THRONE OF GRACE IS ALWAYS ACCESSIBLE to you, especially in your time of need. You can confidently come to Me, knowing that I offer abundant mercy and grace for your daily needs. My throne is merciful and good—not a court of condemnation, but rather one of acceptance and love. I am your good Father, full of grace and mercy. Never fear approaching Me. My Spirit is the Helper and wants to guide you in your time of need.

Heavenly Father, thank You that I can confidently approach You at any time. Help me remember to rely on the Spirit when I find myself in times of need.

Do nothing from selfish ambition or conceit, but in humility count others more significant than yourselves.

PHILIPPIANS 2:3, ESV

A HUMBLE HEART MIRRORS THE HEART OF CHRIST. My ambition for you is selfless living. When you give Me and others credit for your accomplishments, you display humility. Humility is not passivity or insecurity—it's just the opposite. Humility is a confidence and competence that comes from living in the power of the Spirit. I want you to boast, but only boast about My love instead about what you have done. Wrap your conversations in modesty to protect yourself from the pride of wanting to impress. My approval is the best motivation for who you are and what you do.

Heavenly Father, create in me a humble spirit of selfless ambition. Help me to put others first and boast only in Your love.

OCTOBER 23

He knows where I am going.
And when he tests me,
I will come out as pure as gold.

JOB 23:10, NLT

I TEST YOU BECAUSE I LOVE YOU too much to let you remain stagnant. My tests purify your motives. I burn away fleshly thinking, leaving behind a spiritual mind. You are not alone—the Spirit remains with you in the midst of testing. He empowers you to withstand and persevere through any test. Lean into His steadfast leading for direction and support. Testing requires total dependence on Me. There is no test or trial you will face alone because I am always with you. I am faithful.

Heavenly Father, help me to praise You during my tests and trials, knowing You are with me in the middle of them with me. With each test I face, teach me to trust You more.

*If you are offering your gift at the altar and there remember
that your brother or sister has something against you,
leave your gift there in front of the altar. First go and be
reconciled to them; then come and offer your gift.*

MATTHEW 5:23–24

MY WILL FOR YOU IS TO BE RECONCILED when there
is a relational disconnect. Your relationships with others affect your relationship with Me. I humbled Myself
and died on a cross to forgive and reconcile sinners. In
the same way, the Spirit enables and empowers you to
humble yourself by dying to your pride, offering a sincere
apology, and asking for specific forgiveness from someone you have offended. He empowers you to say the right
words in the right way. Remorse and repentance open the
door to relational healing. Seek reconciliation and trust
Me to heal the relationship.

*Heavenly Father, You perfectly modeled forgiveness
and reconciliation to me. Humble my heart to lay aside
pride and ego and seek to be reconciled to those I've
offended.*

Devote yourselves to prayer with an alert
mind and a thankful heart.

COLOSSIANS 4:2, NLT

PRAYER IS A PATHWAY TO PEACE. It's like placing a guard at the gate of your heart to protect against attack. Your heart is the wellspring of life—everything you do flows from it. The Spirit brings order out of chaos and peace out of panic when you spend time with Me in prayer. Prayer aligns your heart with My heart and bends your will toward My will. I use prayer to forgive sin, heal broken hearts, and save lost souls. Prayer is a window into what I am doing in you, others, and the world. Your capacity for gratitude will expand as the Spirit reveals more of Me to you, developing a heart of thanksgiving in you.

Heavenly Father, I praise You for the ability to come to You in prayer. I want my heart to be aligned with You and my will to be bent toward You. Develop in me a heart of gratitude that comes from knowing You.

Since we live by the Spirit,
let us keep in step with the Spirit.

GALATIANS 5:25

I WANT TO SHOW YOU My way for this day. You are prone to live out of your own strength rather than plugging into My power source—the Holy Spirit. He is like the captain of your ship—continually guiding and sustaining you as you navigate through the course of your day. He fills you with love and joy and provides patience and self-control. His kindness, goodness, and gentleness are evident to others when you rely on His power. Keeping in step with the Spirit enables you to live with purpose and peace. Relax in My presence as we move through your day, step by step.

Heavenly Father, I have tried and failed enough to know that I cannot produce spiritual fruit when I live in my own power. I am grateful You don't expect me to live in my own strength. Help me to rely on and keep in step with the Spirit.

We will speak the truth in love,
growing in every way more and more like Christ,
who is the head of his body, the church.

EPHESIANS 4:15, NLT

MY SPIRIT GROWS YOUR RELATIONSHIPS when you speak the truth in love. I flush fear out of your heart when My pure love guides you while you are interacting with others. Pride reacts with harsh, hurtful words, but humility responds with patient, helpful words. Ask the Spirit to guide your words and teach you how to lovingly express what's in your heart. Follow the example of Christ—in humility consider others better than yourself. Choose helpful rather than harmful words so you can build up those around you. Just as I speak life over you, use life-giving words and speak the truth in love.

Heavenly Father, give me a humble heart to loving-ly share the truth with those You love. I want to be a life-giver with my words.

He regarded disgrace for the sake of Christ as
of greater value than the treasures of Egypt,
because he was looking ahead to his reward.

HEBREWS 11:26

MY REWARDS ARE INFINITELY more valuable than any treasures of this world. I reward those who seek Me. Be enamored with Me, not the shiny stuff that will one day tarnish and go away. Ask the Spirit to create contentment in you and to align your heart with Mine. Keep your eyes on the reward of being with Me. Any persecution or disgrace you experience for My sake is of greater value than the treasures of power, prestige, and money. My rewards are priceless!

Heavenly Father, align my heart with Yours and fo-
cus my eyes on the reward that awaits me in eternity.
Create a contentment in me that comes from being in
Your presence.

OCTOBER 29

You are God's children whom he loves, so try to be like him.
Live a life of love just as Christ loved us and gave himself
for us as a sweet-smelling offering and sacrifice to God.

EPHESIANS 5:1–2, NCV

YOU CAN LIVE A LIFE OF LOVE because you are My dearly loved child. In the same way a child imitates their father, you can choose to imitate and express My love through the power of My Spirit. When you love the unlovable, you imitate Me. When you comfort the crushed in spirit, you imitate Me. When you feed the hungry, care for the widow, or tend to the suffering, you imitate Me. When you give generously and sacrificially, you imitate Me. No illness, no financial loss, no rejection, no fear can rob you of My love. You are completely secure in My love, so you can continue to imitate Me in love.

Heavenly Father, give me eyes to see who needs Your love and empower me through Your Spirit to imitate You by living a life of love.

OCTOBER 30

Blessed are those whose ways are blameless, who walk according to the law of the LORD.

PSALM 119:1

I BLESS YOU as you walk in obedience. My beloved child, just as a loving parent provides guidance to protect their loved one from foolishness, I aspire for you to grow in My wisdom. My wisdom is practical and pure, so I can lead you to what's best for you. Meditate, memorize, and reflect on My Word, and the Spirit will illuminate it and lead you into wisdom and understanding. My Word is a lamp for your feet and a light on your path to show you how to walk with Me. With each step you take, you will grow deeper in love with Me.

Heavenly Father, teach me Your Word so I can know You. Guide me and grow me in wisdom so I can walk in Your ways.

When the LORD restored the fortunes of Zion,
we were like those who dreamed. Our mouths were filled
with laughter, our tongues with songs of joy.

PSALM 126:1–2

JOY IS FOUND IN FREEDOM from your captivity to sin. Bondage to your flesh will smother your soul, but My Spirit will set you free and breathe fresh life into your soul. Celebrate your deliverance and the gift of eternal life with Me. Rejoice in My transformative work in your life. Gratitude realigns you to My heart and reminds you of My activity in your life. Make room for the Spirit to fill your heart with My great love, joy, and laughter. I am the giver of freedom and joy. Enjoy the abundant blessing of life with Me.

Heavenly Father, I praise You for the freedom and joy that comes from being Your child. Help me to be a conduit of Your love and freedom to all whose paths I cross.

NOVEMBER

Teach me to do your will,
for you are my God;
may your good Spirit lead
me on level ground.

PSALM 143:10

The LORD is good, a refuge in times of trouble.
He cares for those who trust in him.

NAHUM 1:7

I OFFER COMFORT AND HEALING when you are deceived. When a loved one ceases to love you, cling to My unceasing love. The deep pain of betrayal can cause you to question everything and distrust everyone. Don't allow human failings to deceive you about Me. I am faithful and trustworthy. My Word is reliable and true. The Spirit soothes and consoles you as you find your way to Me. The intense pain of betrayal will lead you into deeper intimacy with Me when you turn to Me rather than bitterness and anger. My unlimited supply of grace and mercy is available to you. Come and rest in My arms.

Spirit of God, lead me into intimacy with the Father rather than holding grudges and becoming angry and bitter. Enable me to extend the same grace and mercy to those who hurt me that You extend to me.

The righteous cry out, and the LORD hears them; he delivers them from all their troubles. The LORD is close to the brokenhearted and saves those who are crushed in spirit.

PSALM 34:17–18

THERE ARE TIMES WHEN YOU FEEL like you are drowning in your troubles. I hear your humble prayers and the cries of your heart. Worry and anxiety often keep you from Me, when it should lead you directly to Me. My Spirit is the answer to your problems, your deliverer from your troubles, and your peace and comfort in your despair. Isolation can make you feel paralyzed and like you have no one to turn to. This is what the Enemy wants—he wants you to feel alone. But I hear your cries, and My Spirit can deliver a supersized portion of comfort and peace. My peace is never-ending, and My comfort is unceasing. I am near to the brokenhearted, and you can be confident that I will deliver you from all your trouble. It may not be immediate, but I am your deliverer.

Heavenly Father, forgive me for running to everyone and everything but You when You are what I need most. Help me to rest in You as wait for You to deliver me.

*The steadfast love of the LORD never ceases; his mercies
never come to an end; they are new every morning; great is
your faithfulness. "The LORD is my portion," says my soul,
"therefore I will hope in him."*

LAMENTATIONS 3:22–24, ESV

HOPE IS FOUND IN ME. My mercies are new every morning. My mercy delivers you from significant losses that
can lead to sorrow. My mercy may extend the life of a
dear friend who is close to death. My mercy helps you
avoid accidents or plans that are not profitable for My
will. The Spirit personifies My mercy, revealing My compassion and grace. Beloved, look for My mercy, see how
much I love you, and watch how I love those you love.

*Heavenly Father, I am so grateful for Your new mercies
every morning—for me and for those I love. My hope
is in You.*

NOVEMBER 4

If I go and prepare a place for you,
I will come back and take you to be with me
that you also may be where I am.

JOHN 14:3

THE WORLD YOU LIVE IN is not My original design. It's
full of suffering and pain, brokenness and shame, and sin
and death. It breaks My heart to see My children hurt
each other and reject Me. I love you with an eternal love,
and I made a way out for you. I eagerly await the day when
I come back for you. I am preparing a place for you—a
place where you can be with Me. When this life feels overwhelming and heavy, turn your eyes toward eternity and
ask the Spirit to overwhelm you with hope—an eternal
hope because I am preparing a place for you.

Heavenly Father, I gratefully anticipate Your prepara-
tions for me now and in the next life. Help me to live
in light of eternity.

Our Father who is in heaven,
hallowed be Your name.
Your kingdom come.
Your will be done,
on earth as it is in heaven.

MATTHEW 6:9–10, NASB

I ANTICIPATE YOUR PRAYERS. As Your Father, I love it when you communicate with Me. I hear your prayers. My Son modeled for you how to pray, and you bless Me when you bow before Me with a humble heart in respect and prayer. Ask the Spirit to direct your prayers according to My will. I long to answer your prayers for My kingdom to come on earth as it is in heaven—it's inviting My power and My will into the details of your life. I can't wait to meet you in prayer.

Heavenly Father, You are holy! I bow before You in worship with a humble heart. May Your kingdom come on earth as it is in heaven.

NOVEMBER 6

The words of the reckless pierce like swords,
but the tongue of the wise brings healing.

PROVERBS 12:18

MY SPIRIT SPEAKS WORDS OF HEALING OVER YOU. In the same way, let your words reflect My Spirit in kindness and gentleness. As the Spirit cultivates a heart of wisdom in you, your words bring comfort, healing, and life to the broken and bruised. When the Spirit guides your speech, it lifts up instead of tearing down. It is full of love instead of hate. It promotes peace instead of turmoil, and it is gentle rather than harsh. Redeeming words full of wisdom, healing, and life flow out of intimacy with Me.

Heavenly Father, thank You for speaking healing words over me. Use my words to bring healing and hope to hurting hearts.

You are the body of Christ,
and each one of you is a part of it.

1 CORINTHIANS 12:27

YOU ARE A UNIQUE PART of the body of Christ, and I will uniquely use you for My glory. The Spirit employs spiritual gifts to show others the way to My irresistible love. Trust the Spirit to give you exactly which gifts are best for you. Be careful not to envy another's gift and dismiss how I have gifted you. You are so special, and I want you to love Me and love people in your unique way. Just as you cherish meaningful material gifts, nurture and cherish your spiritual gifts so I can expand your capacity and grow your influence. The body of Christ is not complete without your part. Use your giftedness to serve others for Me in the power of the Spirit.

Heavenly Father, give me the wisdom and courage to know how to best use my gifts. I count it an honor and privilege to show people the way to Your irresistible love.

NOVEMBER 8

*Jesus said, "You believe because I told you
I saw you under the fig tree.
You will see greater things than that."*

JOHN 1:50

IF YOU CONTINUE TO TRUST ME, I have greater things
for you to see. I have so much more for you, and I want
you to enjoy what I'm doing around you. The Spirit gives
you greater gifts to be used for My purposes—for the
good of others. Don't settle for just seeing what's in front
of you—look around to see My greater things.

*Heavenly Father, give me eyes of faith to see Your
greater work around me. Help me to use the gifts You
entrust to me for the good of others.*

NOVEMBER 9

God did not call us to be impure,
but to live a holy life. Therefore, anyone who rejects this
instruction does not reject a human being but God,
the very God who gives you his Holy Spirit.

1 THESSALONIANS 4:7-8

I DEPOSITED MY HOLY SPIRIT IN YOU to empower you to live a holy life. The Spirit instructs you in My holy ways to prevent you from being swept up in worldly living. My Word instructs you how to reject the impure influences that never stop stalking your life. Praise Me in pure devotion, and the Spirit will create in you a clean heart.

Heavenly Father, protect me from being swept up in worldly living. I receive the fullness of Your Spirit so I can live in a way that is pleasing to You.

You will show me the path that leads to life;
your presence fills me with joy and
brings me pleasure forever.

PSALM 16:11, GNT

LEARNING TO LIVE a life of constant communion and prayer with Me is a process, but I am patient. Conversation with Me fuels your life and clarifies My purpose for you. As you spend more time with Me, you'll recognize your ever-increasing need for Me. I cherish the time we spend together, and I long for you to pour out your heart to Me. My Spirit uses these opportunities to be a balm for your soul—refreshing you before you jump back into your race—and to ignite a passion for Me. Oh, how I passionately love you, My precious one.

Heavenly Father, it is so true—I am fueled for life when I cease running and rest in Your presence. I am grateful You are always patiently waiting for me. Draw me to Yourself in a way that I will not be able to resist.

Rejoice in the LORD and be glad, all you who obey him!
Shout for joy, all you whose hearts are pure!

PSALM 32:11, NLT

MY FACE SHINES UPON YOU and causes gladness in your heart. Gladness—or joy—can be confused with happiness, which is the world's version of joy. It's not the same as the joy My Spirit gives. Happiness ebbs and flows like shifting sand based on circumstances. It's easy for you to be happy when you are in a season of success, prosperity, or fulfillment. However, when you are in the midst of a season of waiting, failure, testing, or stress, you may find it challenging to feel happy. Joy is what you cling to when you are faced with trials and tribulation. My joy transcends human experience. Joy is a fruit of the Spirit and is like a well that never runs dry. It cannot be taken away. It is available even during your darkest hour. My Spirit offers an endless supply of joy, but you must choose to accept it.

Heavenly Father, I can praise You in the middle of a storm because of the power of Your Spirit at work in me. When I confuse joy and happiness and begin to sink in self-pity or hopelessness, remind me that Your joy is a choice that I want to choose each and every day.

When you pray, go into your room, close the door and pray
to your Father, who is unseen. Then your Father,
who sees what is done in secret, will reward you.

MATTHEW 6:6

I HEAR YOU when you pray to Me in secret. It delights Me when you talk to Me throughout the day, but I eagerly await time you dedicate to spend alone with Me. When we are alone, you can more easily focus on Me and listen to the Spirit as He whispers wisdom and life over you. Our time together provides space for you to speak freely to Me and wait for Me to respond. My Spirit settles your soul and clears your mind, bringing you a peace you can't find anywhere else. Come away with Me to a quiet place. I am waiting.

Heavenly Father, nothing is more satisfying than time with You, yet I fill my days with busyness and distractions. I want more of You. Help me to seek You and find You in solitary prayer.

*As God's co-workers we urge you
not to receive God's grace in vain.*

2 CORINTHIANS 6:1

MY GRACE IS NEVER IN VAIN. Grace always accomplishes My purposes through people surrendered to My will. My grace and mercy are unlimited. My grace is the fuel to energize you, and My mercy keeps your relationships running smoothly. Like My Word, My grace does not return void—it facilitates My will. Receive My grace to do My work in the power of My Spirit.

Heavenly Father, I am willing and available to do Your work. Cover me with grace so that I can accomplish Your purposes in the power of the Spirit.

Rejoice always, pray continually, give thanks in all circumstances; for this is God's will for you in Christ Jesus.

1 THESSALONIANS 5:16–18

PRAY WITHOUT CEASING. My will for you is for you to abide in Me and stay in constant communion with Me. When you stay connected to Me through prayer, the Spirit makes it possible for you to rejoice and give thanks in every circumstance. Prayer is a means for ongoing communication with Me, allowing the Spirit to keep your heart and mind in alignment with Me. Stay steady in prayer to remain connected to My life-giving power.

Heavenly Father, help me to stay connected to You through prayer so I can rejoice and give thanks in all circumstances.

Whoever can be trusted with very little
can also be trusted with much.

LUKE 16:10

FAITHFULNESS LEADS TO GREATER OPPORTUNITY. The resources I entrust to you are an opportunity for you to invest in My purposes. I bless you so you can bless others. Extend the same generosity I show you by taking what I give you and putting it to work for My kingdom. As you learn to be faithful with a little, I will expand your capacity to faithfully steward more. Ask the Spirit to open your eyes to ways to model My generosity. May love—not fear—be your motive for managing what I entrust to you.

Heavenly Father, I want to be generous like You. Teach me to be sensitive to ways I can bless others with my time, resources, and talent to invest in what pleases You.

We wait in hope for the LORD;
he is our help and our shield.

PSALM 33:20

MY SPIRIT STRENGTHENS YOUR WEARY SOUL. Everyone is needy—it's just a matter of time before each person must learn to depend on Me. Don't allow divorce, death, or disappointment to isolate you from My love and peace. My Spirit offers comfort and strength as you navigate difficult situations. Your greatest fears may cause you to lose hope. When you place your hope in Me rather than your circumstances, you find peace. The Spirit will calm your fears and lead you securely back to Me. Don't give up on Me or lose hope. I am your hope.

Heavenly Father, strengthen me with a fresh dose of Your life-giving Spirit. Help me to live securely, knowing You alone are my hope.

*God is spirit, and his worshipers must worship
in the Spirit and in truth.*

JOHN 4:24

I DELIGHT IN YOUR WORSHIP. Our time spent together glorifies Me in so many ways. I have no preference of when or where or how you worship. You can talk to Me, sing to Me, kneel to Me, or raise your hands to Me. Simply pour your heart out to Me. You don't have to be in a church or surrounded by a group of believers to honor Me. You can worship Me anywhere, at any time. Time with Me creates a special intimacy between us, providing time and space for you to catch your breath and to put things in your life back into perspective. It's designated time for you to share your heart with Me and listen to the Spirit whisper truth and encouragement into your soul. You need this time with Me as much as I want this time with you.

Heavenly Father, thank You for being so personal to me that I can literally talk to You and worship You wherever I am. Help me to long for time with You each day in such a way that I feel incomplete unless it happens. You are worthy and deserving in every way.

NOVEMBER 18

Each time he said, "My grace is all you need.
My power works best in weakness." So now I am
glad to boast about my weaknesses, so that the power
of Christ can work through me.

2 CORINTHIANS 12:9, NLT

WHERE YOU SEE OBSTACLES, I see opportunities. Your weaknesses are not stumbling blocks for Me because when you are weak, My strength is made perfect. You will face things in your life that will leave you feeling totally incapable or inconsolable. In those times, remember that the Spirit helps you overcome any difficulty you face. Be confident in Me, knowing that the Spirit alone provides the power to overcome. When it feels impossible to take the next step or even to lift your head, remember that you have the Spirit—the Spirit of the Living God—within the very core of your being to give you strength. I will never leave you nor forsake you. You can count on Me with each and every breath. Keep lifting your eyes and looking to Me. I am with you.

Heavenly Father, help me to rely on You when I am weak. Thank You that I can count on You to carry me when I feel as if I can't go any further on my own. When I am weak, You are strong.

We know that in all things God works for the
good of those who love him,
who have been called according to his purpose.

ROMANS 8:28

THERE ARE SOME THINGS IN THIS WORLD that will never be considered good—the unexpected death of a loved one, cancer, addiction, war. Many things will trouble and sadden you, but take heart in My promise that all things work together for good. I will take whatever you are facing and shape it into something beautiful. This doesn't mean everything will work out the way you prefer—it means that in My perfect timing, there will be victory. The victory may not be immediate, but your holiness develops in the process of waiting. My ultimate purpose is to help you become more like Jesus. There is no higher good than this. Trust the Spirit to guide you through whatever you are facing and to mold you into a beautiful image in the very likeness of Jesus.

Heavenly Father, help me to listen for You and to trust You, even in the midst of my darkest days. Thank You for walking before me and behind me and working all things for my good and Your glory.

I will not leave you as orphans;
I will come to you.

JOHN 14:18

I MAKE THE SAME PROMISE TO YOU that I promised My disciples: I will never abandon you. Oh, that you would awaken each morning with a powerful awareness of My Spirit in you. I will carry your burdens, lighten your load, and weaken the pull of familiar temptations on a daily basis. You are no longer a fatherless child—I am your Father! I long to carry you as a baby, to lead you as a child, to guide you, to grow you, and to pour My love and wisdom into you for the rest of your days.

Heavenly Father, my soul rejoices in knowing You are my Father. I cling to Your promise to never abandon me. I adore You, Abba Father.

*The LORD said, "My Spirit will not contend
with humans forever, for they are mortal; their days
will be a hundred and twenty years."*

GENESIS 6:3

I HAVE YOUR LIFE IN MY HANDS. Slow down and rest, knowing that I have numbered your days according to My plan for you. Your life span is in My hands. Where I breathe life, I give life; where I cease to breathe life, I take life and offer eternity. I urge you, My precious child, to inhale My faithfulness and exhale your fears that choke out your hope in Me. Let My Spirit revive your spirit.

Heavenly Father, my life is in Your hands. I trust You with the length of my life and each and every day You give me. Help me to live for You in light of eternity.

You will receive power when the Holy Spirit comes on you;
and you will be my witnesses in Jerusalem, and in all Judea
and Samaria, and to the ends of the earth.

ACTS 1:8

YOU ARE MY WITNESS. I will never leave you powerless as you share My love with others. The moment you place your faith in Me, the Holy Spirit takes up residence in you, constantly nurturing new life in you. Your faith is on display for a watching world. The way you handle trials and tribulation will be evidence of your faith in Me. The Spirit provides a reservoir of power for you to draw upon as you navigate the joys and sorrows of life, and I will use you to draw others into a relationship with Me. Learning to walk in the Spirit's power is an adventure. As our relationship grows, I will continue to work in you, and you will experience abundant life. The Spirit that indwells you makes you a witness for My glory.

Heavenly Father, help me to remember that I can do nothing in my own strength. Give me the wisdom to ask for Your power to be poured out into my life. What an honor it is to be a witness for You to my family, my friends, my community, and to the ends of the earth.

NOVEMBER 23

Our struggle is not against flesh and blood,
but against the rulers, against the authorities,
against the powers of this dark world and against
the spiritual forces of evil in the heavenly realms.

EPHESIANS 6:12

I ASSURE VICTORY. Because of your devotion to Me, some people will resent you, belittle you, and dislike you simply for what you believe. This rejection may hurt, anger, and frustrate you, but make no mistake—these are not your true enemies. Your war is with unseen powers that control this dark world. Satan is the ruler of the earth. He prowls around like a lion and wants to humiliate, shame, and destroy you. He is cunning and deceiving, and he knows your weaknesses. I have won the battle against the Enemy, and the Spirit empowers you to fight the spiritual forces of evil. I provide you with three very powerful weapons that assure victory: My Spirit, My Word, and prayer. Pick up your weapons, use them to overcome the Enemy, and stand firm in My victory.

Heavenly Father, thank You for providing me with the weapons I need to win each battle. Help me to always remember that Satan will make sin look enticing and appealing, but in the end, it leads to my destruction.

*For we are God's masterpiece. He has created
us anew in Christ Jesus, so we can do the good things
he planned for us long ago.*

EPHESIANS 2:10

YOU ARE SET APART. I created you for a unique purpose. Sometimes your purpose will be obvious to you, but there will be times when you must sacrifice comfort and control to discover My will for your life. I will honor the intentional time you set aside to pray and listen to My Spirit for direction. Before you drew your first breath, I prepared good works for you. There will be times when you need to say no to some things in order to say yes to what I've called you to do. Intimate, uninterrupted time spent in prayer and fasting will give you clarity. At times, My will for you will take you out of your comfort zone. Be assured that if I call you to it, I will equip you for it.

Heavenly Father, I praise You for creating me with a special purpose in mind. You have designed me like no other so that I am able to accomplish what You have called me to in order to further Your kingdom. Help me to have an obedient spirit.

Teach me to do your will, for you are my God;
may your good Spirit lead me on level ground.

PSALM 143:10

I AM DRAWN TO WILLING HEARTS. My child, a willing and obedient heart creates intimacy with Me. No one else can teach you what I can teach you and in the way I teach you. My essence is goodness, kindness, and holiness—and it is My very nature to do what's best for you. You can't get to where My Spirit leads on your own. The journey is long and the way is steep. Without Me, you quickly grow weary and faint. But under the Spirit's guidance, the journey is pleasant—without stumbling or wandering. I instruct you in My ways and the Spirit leads you to serenity and security.

Heavenly Father, create in me a willing and obedient heart. Let me see You standing before me with Your hands extended, waiting for me to place my hands in Yours and follow Your lead. Teach me Your ways and lead me to level ground.

Make every effort to keep the unity of the Spirit through the bond of peace.

EPHESIANS 4:3

THERE IS STRENGTH IN UNITY. Backbiting, name-calling, and exclusion are only a few of the tactics the Enemy uses to cause division within the body of Christ. The body of Christ includes My children of all ages, races, social classes, and economic backgrounds. With all the differences, it's easy to lose sight of what you have in common: hope in Me. My Spirit equips you to be humble, gentle, patient, and kind no matter how you are treated. He empowers you to love others with the same kind of love I offer you—unmerited and unconditional. Anything other than unity between My children grieves Me. Division and jealousy are not of Me. Have you been wronged by someone? My child, take the first step toward reconciliation. Do you see strife between family, friends, or coworkers? Step in to help calm the waters. Always be quick to apologize, slow to anger, and generous with encouragement.

Heavenly Father, help me to do my part in keeping the body healthy and whole. Prompt me to forgive others because You have been so faithful to forgive me.

*Don't you know that you yourselves are God's temple
and that God's Spirit dwells in your midst?*

1 CORINTHIANS 3:16

YOU ARE MY BELOVED, and My Spirit lives within you.
The Spirit sustains and guides you in all things and gives
you gifts that allow you to serve others in My name. I
give you a love for others so that you will help them seek
Me. Consistently recognizing My favor and grace in your
life creates a joy in you that is not dependent on your
circumstances. My peace allows you to live in wholeness
and harmony with Me and with others. As you remain
in My presence, I develop patience in you to withstand
challenges with perseverance and endurance. An ever-
present sense of kindness and goodness permeates your
life, giving you a gentleness that sets you apart. Exercise
the gifts of the Spirit and further My kingdom. You are
the only church that some people will ever experience.

*Heavenly Father, oh, what a humbling yet glorious
thought that You live within my soul. Please allow me
to recognize the significance of Your presence and to
use the gifts You give me to draw others to You.*

I am going to send you what my Father has promised; but stay in the city until you have been clothed with power from on high.

LUKE 24:49

I FULFILLED MY PROMISE AND SENT MY HELPER, the Spirit, to live in you. He took up permanent residence in you the day you received salvation. He's always available to you, but you have the option of whether or not you will allow Him to actively control you. The Spirit is your power source and provides you with power to live the life to which I've called you. You can go about your day without plugging into your power source, but you will be unable to resist temptation or produce spiritual fruit. You will exhaust yourself by trying to be good enough, smart enough, and successful enough. You are created to constantly need the Spirit to enable you to live abundantly and obediently. The good news is your power source is always with you.

Heavenly Father, I am in constant need of being clothed by the Spirit. It is impossible to resist temptation when I choose not to live in the Spirit's power. Quicken my spirit when I begin to live in my own strength.

The Spirit God gave us does not make us timid,
but gives us power, love, and self-discipline.

2 TIMOTHY 1:7

MY SPIRIT IS YOUR POWER SOURCE. He supplies you with power to overcome any fear in your life. Do you long to tell others about Me, but find yourself afraid of what they may think or say? Is there a relationship that needs boundaries, but you are reluctant to establish them? Do you shrink from defending your faith? This spirit of timidity is not from Me. The Holy Spirit provides the power and strength to overcome your fears and to resist temptation. He gives you the ability to live in this world but not be of this world. He empowers you to say no to the desires that so easily pull you away from Me. The Spirit enables you to stand strong and firm against the Enemy and to further My kingdom through love and sacrifice. Keep going, My child, for My power and love never run out.

Heavenly Father, when I am reminded of the power You supply me with, I stand strong. You give me every tool I need to overcome my fears and to live for You. Thank You for allowing me to draw from Your strength.

There is therefore now no condemnation to those who are in Christ Jesus, who do not walk according to the flesh, but according to the Spirit.

ROMANS 8:1, NKJV

THE PRIMARY BATTLE YOU FACE is in your mind. You are so harsh on yourself and so easily slip into the pattern of trying to perform for Me. You can't earn My love for you. I love you so much and offer My grace and mercy as a balm to your soul. When faced with temptation, My Spirit offers a way for you to conquer whatever tries to pull you away from Me, and He empowers you to overcome any temptation you face. Listen to My reassuring voice and ask the Spirit to guide you and give you strength to walk in His power. He prevents you from going down a path of pain and destruction and leads you into My safety net full of joy and peace. I don't condemn you, My child. I give you new life in Christ, exchanging a life of sin and death for a life of freedom and grace.

Heavenly Father, sometimes the voice of condemnation is louder than Your voice of grace. Help me to quickly recognize when the Enemy is posing as You so I can silence those thoughts and listen to You.

DECEMBER

*The Spirit God gave us
does not make us timid,
but gives us power,
love, and self-discipline.*

2 TIMOTHY 1:7

DECEMBER 1

*"If I come to the people of Israel and say to them,
'The God of your fathers has sent me to you,' and they
ask me, 'What is his name?' what shall I say to them?'"
God said to Moses, "I AM WHO I AM."*

EXODUS 3:13–14, ESV

I AM WHO I AM. I am the one who will never leave or forsake you. I am the one who rejoices with you in good times and weeps with you in pain. I am the one who longs to replace your despair with peace. I am the one who forgives you. I am your strength when you are weak. I am the one who brings meaning to your pain and trials. I am the one who comforts you in mourning. I am hope for your broken heart. I am the whisper that guides your thoughts. I am the one who deposited the Holy Spirit in you. I am undeniable. I am the one who loves you as you are. I am with you always. I am for you. I am all you need. I AM WHO I AM.

Heavenly Father, You have always been the great I AM, and You always will be. Anchor my soul to Your truth, and teach me to abide in You always. You are all I need.

Be anxious for nothing, but in everything by prayer
and supplication, with thanksgiving, let your requests
be made known to God; and the peace of God,
which surpasses all understanding, will guard
your hearts and minds through Christ Jesus.

PHILIPPIANS 4:6–7, NKJV

CAST ALL YOUR BURDENS ON ME. I want to carry your burdens for you. Run to Me when you are overwhelmed and anxious. Tell Me of your troubles and sorrows. There is no problem too big for Me, no burden too heavy for Me. You are never without the Holy Spirit, your constant companion, who escorts you on your journey. The first step out of darkness is giving thanks. I know this seems contrary to common sense, but I am not common. Praise Me as the storm rages around you. When you take your eyes off your circumstances and fix your eyes on Me, the mystery of My unexplainable, indescribable, supernatural peace overcomes you.

Heavenly Father, lead me to those who need You most,
and give me the courage to open my mouth and allow
Your Spirit to speak through me about Your wondrous
love.

DECEMBER 3

Whatever things are true, whatever things are noble,
whatever things are just, whatever things are pure,
whatever things are lovely, whatever things are of good
report, if there is any virtue and if there is anything
praiseworthy—meditate on these things.

PHILIPPIANS 4:8, NKJV

INTENTLY FOCUS YOUR HEART AND MIND ON ME. As you meditate on My Word and My very essence, you will transcend the frantic and frenetic pace of life and enter into My private presence. It will be just you and Me—no one to distract. Consider who I am and what that means to you personally. I am all-powerful—nothing is too hard for Me. I am all-knowing—nothing takes Me by surprise. I am unchanging—you can always depend on Me. Ask My Spirit to lead you further into My presence and increase your understanding of who I am. I am loving, compassionate, and gracious. I am always with you. I am yours.

Heavenly Father, there is no one like You and nothing like time with You. May the words of my mouth and the meditation of my heart be pleasing in Your sight. You are my Rock and my Redeemer, and I am so grateful I am Your child.

DECEMBER 4

We are therefore Christ's ambassadors, as though God were making his appeal through us. We implore you on Christ's behalf: Be reconciled to God.

2 CORINTHIANS 5:20

YOU ARE MY AMBASSADOR in a hurting world. Rely on My Spirit's presence and power to offer My love and forgiveness to those craving encouragement and hope. Share how My love has changed your life—it is a reminder of My goodness and builds your faith. The Spirit uses your story of My faithfulness to lead others to the joy and freedom of trusting Me. Depend on the Spirit to speak through you—He alone opens the eyes and hearts of those who don't yet know Me. Sharing about My saving grace is a thrilling experience and becomes more natural for you as you learn to let the power of the Spirit work through you. There is no need to feel pressure or tension—you are merely My vessel. Simply share My redeeming love.

Heavenly Father, lead me to those who need You the most, and give me the courage to allow Your Spirit to speak through me about Your wondrous love. Thank You for using me to shine a light for You.

DECEMBER 5

I keep asking that the God of our Lord Jesus Christ, the glorious Father, may give you the Spirit of wisdom and revelation, so that you may know him better.

EPHESIANS 1:17

I LONG FOR YOU TO KNOW ME. Very few people really know Me. I don't want you to merely know *about* Me. I want you to know Me—intimately and personally. I already know your every thought, but I want to be with you and help you get to know Me better with each new day. Intimacy with Me completely transforms your thoughts, actions, and life. Come to Me with your questions, fears, and frustrations. Turn to Me when you are confused, angry, worried, or frightened. The Spirit reveals My immeasurable love for you and leads you into a deeper understanding of who I am. I am gentle and compassionate, and I meet you with kindness. My hope and My power are for you to experience here and now.

Heavenly Father, open my eyes to You. Thank You for dealing gently with me when I bring my requests, doubts, and failures to You. Reveal Yourself to me so that I may know You in ways I don't even realize are possible.

Do not let any unwholesome talk come out of your mouths, but only what is helpful for building others up according to their needs, that it may benefit those who listen.

EPHESIANS 4:29

THE SPIRIT EMPOWERS YOU to speak life into others. He enables you to encourage those around you and share the hope you have found in Me. As you authentically and vulnerably share your life with others, the Spirit works in and through you to lead others to Me. I give you opportunities to allow others to see Me working in your life, and I give you wisdom and confidence when you rely on Me. Let your life be a light for Me.

Heavenly Father, thank You for each and every opportunity You give me to share what You've done for me. Give me the courage to share how You have redeemed me and given me a new life. I am nothing without You.

For who knows a person's thoughts except their own spirit within them? In the same way no one knows the thoughts of God except the Spirit of God.

1 CORINTHIANS 2:11

MY SPIRIT LEADS YOU TO UNDERSTANDING. Slow down and listen for My voice. I want to communicate with you throughout your day. In the same way you can't read the mind or thoughts of others, My thoughts can't be made known to you unless the Spirit reveals them to you. My ways are so very different from human ways. My thoughts may initially seem unreasonable and illogical, but the Spirit imparts My wisdom and understanding. He helps you navigate decisions both big and small. He guides and protects and teaches you to discern My voice. As you begin to trust Me and learn to follow the promptings of the Spirit, you experience peace and joy that can only be found in Me.

Heavenly Father, give me ears to hear and a heart of acceptance. I am humbled that You love me enough to be so personally and intimately involved in my life.

DECEMBER 8

Never be lacking in zeal,
but keep your spiritual fervor, serving the Lord.

ROMANS 12:11

I BRING PURPOSE AND PASSION TO YOUR LIFE. Serving Me brings you joy and contentment, but serving Me in your own strength will exhaust you. Rest in Me and surrender your day to the Spirit to fulfill My work. People who don't know Me can be drawn to My love by even the smallest acts when you serve them with joy—a simple smile showing you care may encourage someone. Becoming bored and lukewarm causes you to be drawn away from Me, signaling that you are working in your own strength. Pause and surrender control to the Spirit, asking Him to renew your zeal and energize you to serve Me. I always provide the power to accomplish what I ask of you.

Heavenly Father, I confess that I oftentimes work in my own strength, which is absolutely futile. Remind me to yield to Your Spirit. Thank You for an endless supply of power to accomplish everything I need to do.

Peter replied, "Repent and be baptized, every one of you,
in the name of Jesus Christ for the forgiveness of your sins.
And you will receive the gift of the Holy Spirit."

ACTS 2:38

MY LOVE CANNOT BE EARNED. You can't work for My love, serve Me for My love, or be good enough for My love. There is nothing you can do to accomplish your salvation. My love is free! The very moment you place your faith and trust in My Son, you receive the gift of the Holy Spirit. You are a new creation! As you walk with Me, the Spirit begins to transform your heart and mind, strengthening your faith. Take advantage of opportunities—like baptism—to share the new life you have in Me. The Spirit supplies you with a new boldness and power in your life to live selflessly and victoriously for Me. The old is gone, the new has come.

Heavenly Father, the fact that salvation is a free gift feels as if it's too good to be true, but that's what makes Your grace so amazing. Help me to live each day in gratitude for what You've done for me.

The Spirit God gave us does not make us timid,
but gives us power, love and self-discipline.
So do not be ashamed of the testimony about our Lord . . .

2 TIMOTHY 1:7–8

DEPEND ON ME when you are challenged to defend your faith. You will find opposition when you share the gospel. Don't be afraid or become discouraged about your ability to communicate My truth. Ask the Holy Spirit to speak through you, and then confidently trust the power of My Spirit. Keep your eyes on Me and allow My Spirit to speak through you. I will empower you with wisdom, discernment, and boldness, and it will be clearly evident that I am working in and through you. Some of My first followers were uneducated fishermen, and they astounded highly educated kings, rulers, and men with their eloquence and power. You can trust Me to do My work through you.

Heavenly Father, I am available to be used by and for You. I reject any fear or distraction from the Enemy that might make me believe I'm unqualified, for the Spirit of the Living God within me is the only credential I need.

I cry out to God Most High,
to God who fulfills his purpose for me.

PSALM 57:2, ESV

YOU PLAY AN INTEGRAL PART IN MY STORY. I write each chapter, weaving the lives of My children together. You play a role that no one else can fulfill. I created you like no one else. I know you intimately—down to the number of hairs on your head. I am keenly aware of your imperfections, but I love you perfectly in spite of them. That's the beauty of My goodness and grace. You don't have to earn My love—in fact, you can't earn it. When you responded in faith to the Spirit revealing Me to you, you received My free gift of eternal life, no strings attached.

Heavenly Father, it is freeing to know that I don't have to work to earn Your love. I rejoice in Your free salvation through Christ. Help me to fulfill Your purpose in my life.

DECEMBER 12

With minds that are alert and fully sober,
set your hope on the grace to be brought to you
when Jesus Christ is revealed at his coming.

1 PETER 1:13

KEEP YOUR EYES ON ETERNITY. I placed a specific yearning for the future within your soul—a longing for the return of Jesus Christ. Every one of your hopes will be fulfilled and your longings satisfied when you are united with Me in eternity. However, in this world, false hopes—money and power and pleasure—so easily distract. They lure you into believing the lies and falling into the traps the Enemy sets to entice you. Money, power, and pleasure are not sinful; they only become an idol when your desire and pursuit of them overshadows your desire and pursuit of Me. The Holy Spirit provides the power and strength you need to combat any temptation. Ask the Spirit to redirect your heart to My ways when you sense the pull to pursue the things of this world instead of Me.

Heavenly Father, help me to live with an eternal perspective, never forgetting the hope that I have in Christ Jesus. Help me to prioritize my thoughts, letting the things of this world become less and less important in my life.

DECEMBER 13

Jesus said to his followers, "Go everywhere in the world, and tell the Good News to everyone."

LUKE 16:15 NCV

YOU ARE A WORLD-CHANGER. I provide opportunities—great and small—for you to assist Me in changing the world. I use you as My hands and feet in the lives of those who need Me. There are so many people longing for the freedom that can only be found in Me, yet they are blind to My truth. Ask Me to show you where I can use you. The Spirit gives you discernment and speaks through you to lead people to Me. Only the Spirit is able to open the eyes of the spiritually blind to find freedom in Christ. Join Me and allow the Spirit to work through you to bring comfort and hope to a hurting and oppressed world.

Heavenly Father, open my eyes today to see the needs of those around me. It is a privilege to share in Your work to bring comfort and freedom to others. Empower me with courage to boldly proclaim Your good news.

As it is written: "What no eye has seen, what no ear has heard, and what no human mind has conceived"—the things God has prepared for those who love him—these are the things God has revealed to us by his Spirit. The Spirit searches all things, even the deep things of God.

1 CORINTHIANS 2:9–10

MY WISDOM IS A MYSTERY that's been hidden since before time began. The Spirit opened your eyes to the knowledge of My saving grace. As you seek Me and grow in knowledge and understanding, the Spirit will continue to reveal My mysteries to you. You will never discover all that I am and all there is to know about Me, for I am beyond your comprehension. But I want you to intimately know Me, and that takes time. You have access to Me every hour of the day—I am always waiting on you to call on Me. And when you do, I will show you more and more of Myself.

Heavenly Father, what an inconceivable privilege to be invited into an intimate relationship with You and be called Your child. Grant me the desire and discipline to spend time with You. I open my heart to You and ask Your Spirit to reveal more and more of You to me.

Jesus called out with a loud voice, "Father,
into your hands I commit my spirit."
When he had said this, he breathed his last.

LUKE 23:46

WHEN YOU ACCEPTED MY REDEEMING LOVE, you committed your spirit to Me forever. But each day, by power of the Spirit, you choose to commit your will to Me with every decision you make. My redemption of your life is far more than an insurance policy inviting you to meet Me in heaven when you die. I desire for you to live this life with passion, purpose, and fulfillment empowered by the Spirit. View life as an adventure and the Spirit as your guide. And when you breathe your last, you will again commit your spirit to Me. Until then, I'm committed to you.

Heavenly Father, lead me into a life with You that is so much more grand than an eternal insurance policy. Help me to choose to live a life of adventure in You—expectant of what the Spirit can accomplish through me when I yield to Him. Thank You for wanting more than a mundane life for me.

We also glory in tribulations, knowing that tribulation produces perseverance; and perseverance, character; and character, hope. Now hope does not disappoint, because the love of God has been poured out in our hearts by the Holy Spirit who was given to us.

ROMANS 5:3–5, NKJV

HOPE IN ME DOES NOT DISAPPOINT. When the pain of taking your next breath overwhelms you, I am with you. The world you live in is fallen—full of sin and decay, sickness and death—and the effects have taken over everything surrounding you. The question isn't will you experience trials and tribulation. The question is, how will you respond? I will carry you through each trial—teaching, restoring, and transforming you with every step. My will in all things is to grow your trust in Me and draw you into a more intimate relationship with Me. And then, by the power and strength of the Spirit, we can begin to walk together in My unfailing love.

Heavenly Father, You uphold me when the pain of life's trials pushes me down. Your hope sustains me when I acknowledge there is purpose in pain. Thank You for using the worst of times as seasons of growth to draw me closer to You.

I am convinced that neither death nor life, neither
angels nor demons, neither the present nor the future,
nor any powers, neither height nor depth, nor anything
else in all creation, will be able to separate us from
the love of God that is in Christ Jesus our Lord.

ROMANS 8:38–39

THIS IS MY PROMISE TO YOU: I love you with an unfailing, unconditional, eternal love. There is nothing you can do or say that will ever prevent Me from loving you. Remain absolutely confident in My love. You are Mine, and nothing can destroy you or separate you from Me. Don't let artificial love prevent you from placing complete faith and trust in My unwavering love for you. My love never leaves or forsakes. When you feel far from Me and lack intimacy, allow the Spirit to lead you back to Me. I wait for you with open arms. Even death won't separate us—in fact, it will eternally unite us. You have nothing to fear.

Heavenly Father, thank You for the assurance of Your
perfect love. Your love casts out all fear and holds me
securely. Call me into Your loving presence when I be-
gin to drift and fill me with Your love and peace.

Do not worry about tomorrow, for tomorrow will worry about itself. Each day has enough trouble of its own.

MATTHEW 6:34

WORRY IS AN OBSTACLE TO FAITH. Worry and anxiety weigh you down and cause you to question Me. Call upon the Spirit to remind you that I have never failed you. I know how easy it is for you to linger in worry, focusing on your burdens. I long to lift the weight of your burdens from your shoulders. Bring them to Me, and the Spirit will exchange your anxious thoughts for peace. I am gentle and humble; I listen to your concerns and offer comfort. I am always here for you. Nothing will ever separate you from My love. Exchange your worry for My peace, and trust Me with your days.

Heavenly Father, thank You for Your peace in exchange for my worry. I trust You with all of my days. Help me to focus on You when my worries threaten to drown out Your truth.

DECEMBER 19

If we confess our sins, he is faithful and just and will forgive us our sins and purify us from all unrighteousness.

1 JOHN 1:9

FORGIVENESS FOLLOWS YOUR CONFESSION. There is no need to distance yourself from Me after you've sinned. The world you live in is fallen, and I know you are bombarded with temptations all day, every day. I don't expect you to be perfect. In fact, I knew you wouldn't be, and I knew you couldn't be. You see, My child, I foreknew that humanity would rebel and disobey Me. That's what's so amazing about My grace. I knew you would choose disobedience over Me. But that didn't matter—I still created the world and everything in it for My pleasure and for your pleasure, knowing I would have to make the ultimate sacrifice and pay your debt for sin. I have no regrets. You are worth it to Me. I bought you back, and you are Mine forever.

Heavenly Father, I confess that there are areas of my life that I have not completely given over to You. Shine Your purifying light on those dark areas of my heart so that I can turn them over to You. Thank You for Your forgiveness and for cleansing me from all unrighteousness.

Rejoice always, pray continually,
give thanks in all circumstances;
for this is God's will for you in Christ Jesus.

1 THESSALONIANS 5:16–18

DELIGHT IN ME, for I am an unending supply of joy. Live in total dependence on Me by communicating with Me spontaneously and frequently. Set aside time each day to be with Me, and also keep a conversation going with Me throughout your day. The Spirit empowers you to maintain a heart of gratitude because I am in control and work all things out for your good and My glory. Lean into Me and keep Me in the forefront of your thoughts and ideas—big and small. Share your innermost thoughts and feelings with Me. Nothing is off-limits when you pray— no question, burden, or idea. I long for My Spirit to communicate with you to reveal more of who I am so you can know Me more intimately.

Heavenly Father, I'm amazed that You have a desire to continually communicate with me. Keep me close to You, and protect me from distractions that can so easily cause me to forget to connect with You. Teach me to live in utter dependence on You.

DECEMBER 21

*Martha was distracted by all the preparations
that had to be made. She came to him and asked,
"Lord, don't you care that my sister has left me
to do the work by myself? Tell her to help me!"*

LUKE 10:40

BUSYNESS IS THE ENEMY OF INTIMACY BETWEEN US.
The birth of Jesus is certainly reason to celebrate, but be
careful not to miss the gift of it. Spend time wrapped
in My presence rather than spending time impeccably
wrapping gifts. Free yourself from the burden of perfection and frantic preparations. Rest in My perfect love.
Slow down and savor the true gift I sent you—My Son.
Ponder what this really means for you. Ask the Spirit to
further open your heart to Me. Because of My great love
for you, I sacrificed what's most important to Me to build
a bridge to your heart. That's how much you are worth to
Me! So don't worry if every detail has been attended to.
Only one thing is needed: time with Me.

*Heavenly Father, there is no other gift like Jesus.
You're all I want and all I need. Help me choose what's
better when I'm tempted to get caught up in busyness
because You are best.*

This is how the birth of Jesus the Messiah came about:
His mother Mary was pledged to be married to Joseph,
but before they came together, she was found to be
pregnant through the Holy Spirit.

MATTHEW 1:18

I AM LIFE-GIVING. I create life—precious life—with a word. The Spirit came on Mary—a virgin—and My power brought forth the life of My Son, Jesus. Jesus was born not to live, but to die. He was born to die on a cross as payment for your sin to take away your shame and guilt. When you surrendered and gave your life to Jesus, He created new life in you. Human effort can take no credit for your spiritual conversion. I chose you before you even knew Me. I gave life to you, and you are My precious, beloved child. I will love you and lead you all the days of your life.

Heavenly Father, nothing is impossible for You. When I begin to doubt You, remind me that Jesus was born of a virgin. Nothing can thwart Your plan for mankind or Your purpose for my life. I rest in Your absolute control.

She gave birth to her firstborn, a son.
She wrapped Him in cloths and placed Him in a manger,
because there was no guest room available for them.

LUKE 2:7

WHEN MY SON CAME INTO THE WORLD, there was no room for Him. He was born into a humble family dealing with the disgrace of an unwed mother. No one expected Him to arrive as He did. No one recognized Him as anything other than a baby born into poverty, but I sent Him for you. Don't miss Him, beloved, for He gives you direct access to Me. I show up in the middle of messes, like messy relationships and family situations. I can be found in the least likely places, with the sinners rather than the religious. I make room for you when others push you out. I came to live with you—to make a way for you. I came to save you. My love has room for you.

Heavenly Father, I am overwhelmed by Your love and saving grace. Show up in my messy relationships and lead me to reconciliation. Let me see You in the least likely places and offer Your grace and forgiveness. You are my Wonderful Counselor, Mighty God, Everlasting Father, and Prince of Peace.

The virgin will conceive and give birth to a son, and they will call him Immanuel (which means, "God with us").

MATTHEW 1:23

I AM WITH YOU. Don't be afraid when I conceive ideas in your heart that seem surreal or too fantastic for you. My Spirit specializes in leading you into unknown and unfamiliar territory so you are able to experience My presence in a deeper, more meaningful way. Fear or lack of faith may cause you to hesitate, but lean into My love instead. I am with you to share My gift of love through you.

Heavenly Father, give me the wisdom to recognize when You are conceiving seemingly impossible ideas in my heart and help me to trust the Spirit to lead me in the unknown. The safest place I can be is in the center of Your will.

DECEMBER 25

She will give birth to a son,
and you are to give him the name Jesus,
because he will save his people from their sins.

MATTHEW 1:21

JESUS WAS BORN A MAN so that you could be born again spiritually. I sent My Son to earth to save you from your sin because of My great love for you. Some wanted a King, but Jesus came to reign over your heart with My peace. I long to shepherd your soul with My loving-kindness and long-suffering. During this busy time of year, slow down and celebrate My gift of salvation. Make room for My Spirit to work in your life. Christmas is My gift of love and forgiveness to you.

Heavenly Father, reign over my life and cover me in Your perfect peace. Help me to live in light of Your great love and forgiveness and to never get over the gift of Your salvation.

Nor do I count my life dear to myself,
so that I may finish my race with joy,
and the ministry which I received from the Lord Jesus,
to testify to the gospel of the grace of God.

ACTS 20:24, NKJV

I MADE YOU ON PURPOSE with a mission to make Me known. Everything else you do is extra. Knowing your purpose is what gives meaning to life. It keeps you from feeling pushed and pulled in so many directions. Anchor your life on the mission to make Me known, and it will simplify life for you. My Spirit living through you opens doors and opens hearts for you to make Me known. You can make Me known at work or at a sporting event. You can make Me known to your neighbors and your community. You can make Me known to your family and friends. You can make Me known no matter where you are. I created you to make Me known.

Heavenly Father, life really doesn't have to be compli-
cated. If I simply invite You in wherever I go and allow
Your Spirit to flow out of me, I will make You known.
There is no greater privilege than to display Your glory.
Help me to live with an eternal perspective, focusing
on what matters to You.

*I also pray that you will understand the incredible
greatness of God's power for us who believe him.
This is the same mighty power that raised Christ from
the dead and seated him in the place of honor at God's right
hand in the heavenly realms.*

EPHESIANS 1:19, NLT

MY POWER IS AVAILABLE to you when you face such overwhelming challenges that you aren't capable of mustering enough personal strength and courage to handle them. You were never meant to handle these burdens alone. The Spirit inhabits you to strengthen and empower you to walk through any trial you face. In times of distress, call on the Spirit and ask for an extraordinary measure of His power. My presence provides the strength you need for daily battle. I am here for you, and I will not leave you. Rest in My presence and experience the peace only I offer.

Heavenly Father, give me the power and strength I need to remain faithful. I am grateful that You will never leave me and that I am not meant to carry my burdens alone.

DECEMBER 28

The Spirit gives life; the flesh counts for nothing.
The words I have spoken to you—they are full
of the Spirit and life.

JOHN 6:63

MY SPIRIT GIVES LIFE. Not just life for today, but eternal life. Many share words that are appealing and sound wise, but words spoken in the flesh count for nothing. They leave you empty and cause you to work harder to achieve success. On the contrary, My Word leads you to life. The Spirit opens the eyes of your heart and leads you to Me. He enables you to have faith in Me made possible through Jesus. There is nothing you can do to earn My love. It's a free gift from Me, no strings attached. I gave My all to get you—that's how much I love you!

Heavenly Father, I praise You for opening my eyes to truth and leading me into a relationship with You. Thank You for the gift of eternal life.

DECEMBER 29

You know when I sit and when I rise; you perceive my thoughts from afar. You discern my going out and my lying down; you are familiar with all my ways. Before a word is on my tongue you, Lord, know it completely.

PSALM 139:2–4

MY SILENCE DOES NOT SIGNIFY MY ABSENCE. When your emotions begin to get ahead of you and you feel like I am distant, don't assume I've abandoned you. When you have difficulty hearing My voice, don't assume I'm uninterested or uninvolved. I am fully aware of every detail of your life—down to the number of hairs on your head. I know everything about you. I know your thoughts before you think them and your words before you speak them. I know all there is to know and all that can be known. I am in complete control. I arrange the people, places, and events in your life to work for your good. You are never alone—My Spirit lives *in* you, which means I'm always with you. I will *never* leave you.

Spirit of God, keep me in perfect peace when my emotions get out of control. Remind me that my Father knows every detail of my life and is in complete control.

DECEMBER 30

Create in me a pure heart, O God,
and renew a steadfast spirit within me.

PSALM 51:10

I WIPE YOUR HEART CLEAN. I am a safe place for you to share your struggles, and I offer forgiveness, mercy, and compassion. As you express your regrets and how you fall short, I listen with tenderness and compassion. My Son gave His life for you so that you don't have to suffer from guilt and condemnation. My mercies are new every morning. I create a pure heart in you and give you a clean slate to begin each day. My Spirit restores your joy and gives you a heart of thanksgiving as He develops an unwavering faith in you. I desire for you to fully live in My grace, love, and forgiveness by the power of the Spirit.

Heavenly Father, wipe my heart clean with Your purifying forgiveness. Renew my heart and mind, and give me an unwavering faith to follow You all the days of my life.

I am the Lord your God who takes hold of your right hand and says to you, Do not fear; I will help you.

ISAIAH 41:13

MY HELP IS NECESSARY to live a fulfilling life. Your life is like a ship on an open sea. You will navigate through calm, rough, uncertain, and beautiful waters. If the Spirit is the source of your strength, you will not grow tired as you navigate each season. Faith in Me triumphs over fear and the frustration you feel when you realize your helplessness. I am always available—simply bring your hopes, dreams, and burdens to Me and allow Me to lead you toward wisdom, peace, and courage. As you trust Me with your life and the lives of those you love, I will show My loving faithfulness to you.

Heavenly Father, I desire an abundant and fulfilling life that brings You glory. I am wholly dependent on Your Spirit to help me navigate each season of my life. Lead me to a life of complete surrender and trust in You.

EPILOGUE

Nicodemus was a religious leader who met with Jesus to discuss His teachings. Nicodemus inquired, "How can someone be born when they are old?" Jesus responded: "Very truly I tell you, no one can enter the kingdom of God unless they are born of water and the Spirit. Flesh gives birth to flesh, but the Spirit gives birth to spirit. You should not be surprised at my saying, 'You must be born again.' The wind blows wherever it pleases. You hear its sound, but you cannot tell where it comes from or where it is going. So it is with everyone born of the Spirit." (John 3:4-8)

As Jesus explained, the Spirit calls lost souls to be born again into the kingdom of heaven. The Holy Spirit indwells humble hearts to comfort, teach, guide, and glorify. The Spirit is calling and has something to say to you.

Spirit Calling to Comfort You

The Holy Spirit comforts hurting hearts. His comfort heals your soul, and He alone is able to enter into the depths of despair and replace loneliness with His presence and perfect love. The Spirit's tender compassion comforts the wounds your heart suffers with the gentleness of a mother comforting her hurting child. He freely offers mercy and love to soothe your aching soul. The Spirit calls you and offers the blessing of comfort for your heart.

Spirit Calling to Teach You

The Holy Spirit lights your way and leads you in the path of righteousness. Just as a loving parent instructs a child flirting with foolishness, the Spirit pricks your conscience to flee from sin and faithfully follow the Lord. He waves a warning flag over unwise decisions with tough and tender love. The Spirit's conviction stings in the moment but prevents future pain. He teaches you to walk in righteousness and to live an abundant life. The Spirit teaches you because He loves you, and as you learn from Him, you will grow in perfect love.

Spirit Calling to Guide You

The Holy Spirit is your spiritual guide, leading you into truth and helping you discern the countless decisions you face. Your spirit seeks discernment to grow in grace into the likeness of Christ. The Spirit will tutor you in wisdom as you surrender to His guidance, and He will guide you and give you understanding into eternal truths.

Spirit Calling to Glorify God

The Holy Spirit is humble and does not draw attention to Himself. Everything the Spirit does is for the glory of God. He leads you into worship and unfiltered praise and glory—a glory reserved only for God, the Lord of lords and the King of kings!

By the power of the Spirit,
Boyd Bailey

Seeking God's Heart

365-DAY DEVOTIONAL

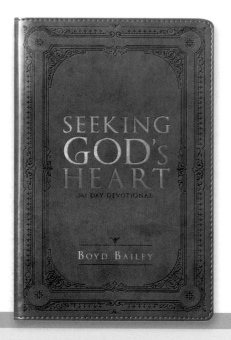

Seeking God's Heart is a 365-day devotional. Each day is Scripture-based and designed to take 3 minutes to get you into a daily habit of meeting with God.

Spirit Calling to Teach You

The Holy Spirit lights your way and leads you in the path of righteousness. Just as a loving parent instructs a child flirting with foolishness, the Spirit pricks your conscience to flee from sin and faithfully follow the Lord. He waves a warning flag over unwise decisions with tough and tender love. The Spirit's conviction stings in the moment but prevents future pain. He teaches you to walk in righteousness and to live an abundant life. The Spirit teaches you because He loves you, and as you learn from Him, you will grow in perfect love.

Spirit Calling to Guide You

The Holy Spirit is your spiritual guide, leading you into truth and helping you discern the countless decisions you face. Your spirit seeks discernment to grow in grace into the likeness of Christ. The Spirit will tutor you in wisdom as you surrender to His guidance, and He will guide you and give you understanding into eternal truths.

Spirit Calling to Glorify God

The Holy Spirit is humble and does not draw attention to Himself. Everything the Spirit does is for the glory of God. He leads you into worship and unfiltered praise and glory—a glory reserved only for God, the Lord of lords and the King of kings!

By the power of the Spirit,
Boyd Bailey

Seeking God's Heart
365-DAY DEVOTIONAL

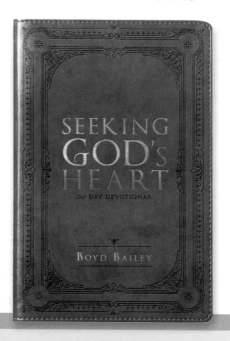

Seeking God's Heart is a 365-day devotional. Each day is Scripture-based and designed to take 3 minutes to get you into a daily habit of meeting with God.

Wisdom for Living
40-DAY DEVOTIONAL

Wisdom for Living is a 40-day devotional designed to introduce to you core principles to learn how to walk in wisdom with the Lord.